mountains
and marshes

mountains and marshes

exploring the bay area's natural history

David Rains Wallace

COUNTERPOINT | BERKELEY, CALIFORNIA

Library of Congress Cataloging-in-Publication Data Is Available

Cover design by Kelly Winton
Interior design by Elyse Strongin, Neuwirth & Associates, Inc.
Illustrations by Lucy Conklin
Map © David Rumsey Map Collection, www.davidrumsey.com

ISBN 978-1-61902-596-7

Counterpoint Press
2560 Ninth Street, Suite 318
Berkeley, CA 94710
www.counterpointpress.com

Printed in the United States of America
Distributed by Publishers Group West

10 9 8 7 6 5 4 3 2 1

contents

It is, I find, in zoology as it is in botany:
all nature is so full, that that district produces
the most variety that is most examined.

—GILBERT WHITE
The Natural History of Selborne

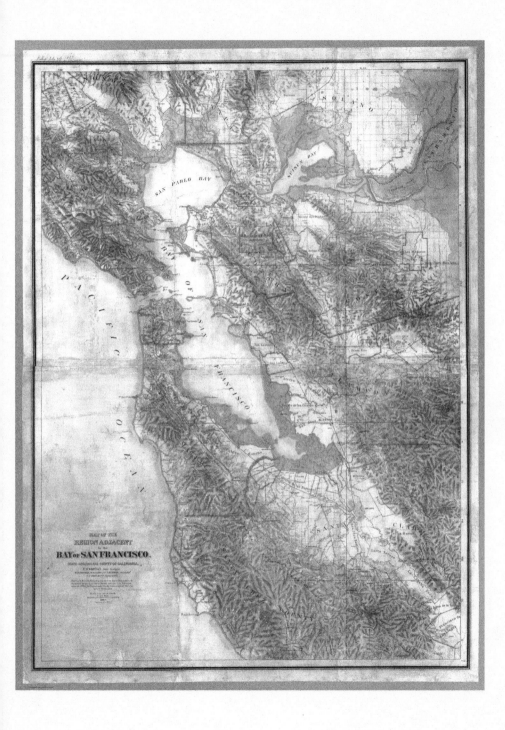

MAP OF THE
REGION ADJACENT
to the
BAY of SAN FRANCISCO.

mountains
and marshes

the serpentine gate

Like other large bodies of water, San Francisco Bay takes on every color at some time, from black at midnight to white at noon. To me, the most characteristic one is a milky bluish green that I see on summer evenings when I cross the Richmond Bridge going east. There is a sense of celestial depth about it, paradoxical as that might be. It seems very alive after the baked brown of the inland hills.

It is the color of serpentine, which is appropriate. Serpentine is a common rock around the Bay Area, but a strange one. It comes from earth's mantle, a hot layer of heavy metals many miles beneath the surface, and it reaches the sunlight only after millions of years of geological processes that would be cataclysmic if they weren't so slow.

Huge plates that form the planet's crust collide and slide against each other, dragging slabs of the underlying mantle along. When one plate rides over another in the tectonic process called subduction, mantle material scrapes onto earth's surface, forming an igneous rock called peridotite, which weathers to red or black. But some mantle material mixes with water during subduction, forming a metamorphic rock that weathers a slick, milky bluish green at the surface. It is called serpentine because its color and texture seem snakelike.

Some serpentine further metamorphoses into jade, a semiprecious stone thought to have magical properties. Serpentine has its own magical property. Because of its heavy metal chemistry, its soil resists the weedy exotic vegetation that has preempted much of the Bay Area, allowing many beautiful native plants and the animals that depend on them to survive. For plants that have been evolving here for millions of years to persist on rock that has been forming for an estimated 200 million years seems to embody the evolutionary nature of this place. And for that rock to be associated with the serpent, the creature that—more than most—connects with the depths of earth and time, seems to embody the Bay Area's mythic nature. It's easy to imagine some sinuous ridgetop of slick blue-green rock as a coil of a snake, so big and old that its movements are too slow for human perception—a World Serpent.

The Golden Gate is a misnomer in geological terms. The only natural gold I know of in the Bay Area is the residue of Mother Lode mining scraps that rivers have washed into the Bay. It's really the Serpentine Gate.

Of course, the Chamber of Commerce wouldn't like calling it that. Prejudice against serpents and anything associated them has been endemic to Western civilization since Genesis. Prejudice persists even in these "green" times. The illustrator of my book *The Klamath Knot* made a wonderful jacket design of a World Serpent coiled around the Klamath Mountains. But market research at Sierra Club Books rejected it for a less inspiring one of an anthropomorphic myth, the giant Bigfoot.

The prejudice is recent. Most cultures, including Western ones, have revered snakes because of their associations with depths and origins. The ancient Greek oracles and Eleusinian mysteries centered on snakes. The greatest prophetess, the Delphic oracle, was the Pythoness. Many learned volumes have been written about snake mythology. But the most interesting way into snake lore is through the snakes themselves, preferably the local ones.

The Bay Area isn't the snake capital of the world. It doesn't, for one thing, have green snakes, the color that people archetypically associate with them. (Children usually color snakes green.) The local rattlesnake's scientific name used to be *Crotalus viridis,* the green rattler, and although there are greenish rattlers in the West, Bay Area ones I've seen are brownish or reddish. The only remotely green snake here is the racer, which can be olive drab when it's not plain brown.

Archetypes aren't everything, however, and the Bay Area may be the snake capital of the West Coast. Species from all over converge on our convenient location and salubrious climate, about equally divided among ones with northern, eastern, and southern affinities. Roughly two dozen species live here, although it's hard to be sure because snakes are such cryptic, supple creatures. Legless crawlers may seem primitive, but fossils show that snakes are the most recently evolved of major vertebrate groups, appearing about 100 million years ago, after mammals and birds. Evolution often diversifies by simplifying: snakes have traded legs for a versatile niche in the interstices of things. And they can be hard to find there. In five decades of hiking around the Bay Area, I haven't seen all the species thought to live here.

Only one species is really commonplace, like deer or quail. That is the gopher snake, the medium-sized tan-and-brown-mottled species that stretches lazily across paths even in the Berkeley Hills. It is an easygoing snake when mature, although little ones can be bratty, striking and vibrating their tails at passersby. I suppose one reason gopher snakes are so common and good-natured is that they are well fed: they eat an abundant variety of small mammals, including gophers.

Garter snakes are North America's most common snakes, but there are so many species that it's hard to know which you're seeing. The Bay Area has three, but there are several subspecies and an impossible tangle of common names. Most garter snakes have yellow stripes, but two species here also have other colors. One of these, *Thamnophis sirtalis*, has red stripes or blotches—and often a blue belly. It is common in terrestrial habitats, although a subspecies, the San Francisco garter snake, is endangered. Another common species, *T. elegans,* has red stripes or blotches—rarely a blue belly—and lives in similar places. The other Bay Area species, *T. atratus*, has only yellow stripes and is common in aquatic habitats. The two terrestrial species may frequent water too, however. Garter snake identification is just a mess, although stripe color sometimes helps. Happening once on a garter snake eating tadpoles of the endangered red-legged frog, I knew it wasn't one endangered species eating another because it had only yellow stripes.

Bay Area garter snakes, at least some of them, have one uncommon talent. Snakes are of course notorious for injecting poison with hypodermic fangs, although most don't have poison or hypodermic fangs. But garter snakes here are famous for their ability to *digest* the virulently poisonous bodies of two local salamander species, the California and rough-skinned newts, which can contain enough toxins in their skins to kill multiple humans. Bay Area newts are the most poisonous on the West Coast, and they may have become so in an "arms race" with Bay Area garter snakes.

The Pacific rattlesnake is the only other species I've seen here very often. In protected areas like Mount Diablo, rattlesnakes can be almost as visible as gopher snakes, and they have similar lazy dispositions in my experience, although I've never deliberately gotten close enough to test this. (Rattlesnake venom seldom kills humans, but an envenomed bite is very painful and may cause lasting damage to tissue.) I've accidentally walked within a foot or two of some and gotten no response. I've never even provoked a rattle here. The snakes just crawl away. I've used a pole to coax rattlers off roads a few times, and they don't coil or strike, just feint irritably at the pole before departing.

Perhaps Bay Area rattlesnakes are phlegmatic because, like gopher snakes, they have plentiful food sources, especially California ground squirrels. Rattlesnakes live on such close terms with the squirrels—in their tunnels—that adults may be immune to rattlesnake venom, having survived a bite or two. Rattlers mainly eat young squirrels, although adults defend their babies by kicking sand or waving their tails at them. Females rub shed snake's skins on themselves and their babies, thus confusing the rattlers' sensory organs.

Maybe some rattlesnakes here have just given up bothering about people because there are so many of us wandering around. Once, unwisely climbing a steep grassy slope off-trail, I came face to face with a rattler in a squirrel hole under a rock overhang, and it didn't blink (figuratively speaking, that is—snakes don't have eyelids). It didn't even flick out its tongue, the serpentine version of curiosity. If a snake could have an expression, I would say it looked resigned.

The only rattlesnake bite recipient of my acquaintance was a scientist with a captive specimen. Still, it's hard to convince people that rattlers are statistically far below bathtubs on the danger scale. Their Genesis voltage remains high enough to boil the brains of a cool customer like Joan Didion as she muses on her Sacramento Valley family cemetery in *Where I Was From*:

> When I was in high school and college and later I would sometimes drive out there, park the car and sit on the fender and read, but after the day I noticed, as I was turning off the ignition, a rattlesnake slide from a broken stone into the dry grass. I never again got out of the car. . . .
> I had seen the rattlesnake but I had failed to get out of the car

and kill it, thereby violating, in full awareness that I was so doing, what my grandfather had told me was "the code of the West."

The most disturbing snake experience I've had in the Bay Area wasn't with a rattlesnake but with a common king snake, which, because it preys higher on the food chain than gopher snakes and rattlesnakes (in fact, on gopher snakes and rattlesnakes), is less numerous. I was at a stable getting manure for a garden when the bottom of the hole I was digging suddenly turned into a big black-and-white-banded snake. It didn't do anything except crawl deeper into the dung heap, but the surprise was dizzying. There's something powerfully chthonic about a black-and-white-banded snake, and I've always felt a frisson about seeing king snakes emerge from the ground, which is how I've usually—albeit infrequently—seen them.

Ted Hughes, English poet laureate from 1984 to 1998, evokes this in a poem about a 1959 trip across America:

WE CAME TO A STONE

Beside a lake flung open before dawn
By the laugh of a loon. The signs good.
I turned the stone over. The timeless one,
Head perfect, eyes waiting—there he lay
Banded black,
White, black, white, coiled. I said
"Just like the coils on the great New Grange lintel."
One thing to find a guide.
Another to follow him . . .

—*"The Badlands"*

King snakes' rattler diet certainly gives them cachet. And they are beautiful snakes. I think the other king snake species that occurs in the Bay Area, the mountain king snake, is the most beautiful snake in the West. It is banded black, white, black, red, black, white—as Ted Hughes might have described it. But I haven't seen it here.

I've seen ring-necked snakes here about as often as common king snakes, although that's not necessarily proof of rarity. One study estimated a population of nine hundred ring-necked snakes in an area the size of a football field. They are pretty little snakes, maximum length about three feet, with orange or yellow neck rings and bluish bodies. A smaller local snake may be even more numerous, although it's hard to tell because it's even less visible. The sharp-tailed snake is the smallest I've seen here, eighteen inches maximum, and it spends most of its sedentary life underground, emerging at night to eat slugs.

The strangest snake I've encountered in the Bay Area is the rubber boa, which, as its name implies, belongs to the group that includes pythons, anacondas, and boa constrictors, the ultimate World Serpents. Rubber boas are even more archetypical than giant pythons because they are a relict of the late dinosaur age—long before gopher snakes and rattlesnakes. They are as efficient at constricting their prey as their big relatives: Harry Greene, a snake expert formerly at UC–Berkeley, recorded one individual that had just eaten three moles. Their maximum length is thirty inches, however, so they tend to be overlooked. I thought a foot-long one that I encountered on the Coast Trail at Point Reyes National Seashore was a piece of brown-and-yellow bungee cord until I picked it up. Then it coiled and gripped my finger with a pair of little legs on its rear end. Boas show their evolutionary age by being the only snakes with such vestigial legs, which they use not to get around but to grip sexual partners.

I once dreamt of digging up a rubber boa so big that it curled all the way around a backyard garden. At least, its head was at one end and its tail at the other: I couldn't see how much more of it there was, and I couldn't decide whether to dig up more of it or to start burying it again. There was a sense of danger in this, but also of exhilaration and, somehow, reassurance. This had to do with a series of brilliantly marked birds that landed on a bare sapling in mid-garden and then zoomed away again—a crimson-black-and-white sapsucker, a scarlet-yellow-and-black western tanager, and a black-and-white poorwill. Since poorwills are actually grayish-brown, nocturnal birds that perch on the ground, the latter seemed particularly significant for some reason.

There is a group that I'm not sure about because they are so fast. I may have seen a racer or a striped racer, but all I could see was sinuous bodies slipping through chaparral or grass. I could be pretty sure it wasn't an Alameda striped racer, a subspecies of the latter, since it is endangered. I did have an impressive sighting of another possible Bay Area member of this group—a big purplish snake called the coachwhip—but not here. It appeared so suddenly before my car at a freeway overpass south of Joshua Tree National Park that there seemed no way not to hit it, but when I stopped and looked, it had disappeared. Harry Greene observed that coachwhips "almost defy the laws of physics at times."

The snakes I'm sure I haven't seen are those specializing in the dry habitats of the eastern Bay Area. That is the remotest and most trashed part, between agribusiness, wind and solar farms, and hazardous research or industrial facilities. The best-known arid reptile habitat, Corral Hollow, is the site of a state vehicular recreation area, and then there was the Altamont Speedway from 1966 until it closed in 2008. Having endured the 1968 Rolling Stones concert there, I can testify to its ecological grimness. Even in protected areas like Round Valley Regional Preserve near Brentwood—actually one of the most beautiful landscapes here—local snakes are elusive because arid land species largely live to beat the heat, emerging at night.

There are four such species known here. The California night snake, the size of a garter snake, is the Bay Area's other poisonous snake, subduing its frog or lizard prey with venom from enlarged teeth on the back of its upper jaw. It's not dangerous to humans, so it doesn't have a rattlesnake's charisma. The California black-headed snake is smaller than the sharp-tailed snake and stays underground more. The glossy snake is a smaller, paler relative of the gopher snake. The long-nosed snake is a drabber relative of the mountain king snake.

If this was PBS *Nature*, I'd proceed to lecture about how all snakes are threatened everywhere. And it's true enough in the megalopolis. Even in parks, mountain bicyclists who insist on illegally riding foot and horse trails kill snakes—I've found the bodies. Some people deliberately kill snakes just because they don't like them, which humans probably always have done, reverence or not. Apollo, god of arts and sciences, slew the primordial Great Python, although the corpse just came apart and crawled away to become the local ones of rites and oracles.

> . . . a gigantic serpent.
> Python by name, whom the new people dreaded,
> A huge bulk on the mountain side. Apollo,
> God of the glittering bow, took a long time
> To bring him down . . .

In memory of this, the sacred games
Called Pythian, were established . . .

—*Ovid, Metamorphoses*

There are interesting questions as to why snakes are threatened. Much native wildlife has adapted to urban living—mostly birds and mammals but some "herptiles" too. Salamanders abound in gardens; frogs and turtles survive around creeks and ponds; I've seen a native fence lizard in my North Berkeley neighborhood. But I've never seen a snake—not even the most common or most secretive kind. (Given their slug diet, little sharp-tailed snakes should be welcome garden residents and may persist in some suburban backyards, but not mine.) Cats, rats, and cars must have a lot to do with this. Sun-warmed roads are narcotic for night-roaming snakes. Still, it's puzzling that a group that succeeds in so many other hostile environments should fail in this one.

Maybe they just need time to adapt. Snakes are slow, comparatively speaking, but so is evolution. Another interesting aspect of Bay Area snakes is that competitive exotic species and diseases don't seem to have impacted them. Introduced mammals, birds, plants, turtles, and frogs have run riot, but I know of nothing here like the situation with escaped Burmese pythons in Florida, although pet owners must release or lose many exotic snakes here every year. I've never seen a feral exotic snake here, anyway. Maybe, where they do survive, native snakes have filled the ecological niches so efficiently that intruders can't get in.

Civilization certainly has changed the Bay Area in the past two centuries with its wonders like the Golden Gate Bridge. Some say that it has "transformed" the place and proclaim an "end of nature." That is nonsense. According to probability math, what has lasted longest will last longest. So it's 100 million years of snakes against five thousand years of bridges. And of course the World Serpent of our blue-green ridges is not always imperceptibly slow in its movements.

Vita longia, ars brevis.

the bay west

harbor seals

It is a windy December day: the water beneath the rowboat looks excessively cold and briny. With a lonesome awareness of my dependence on land, I turn to see how far I am from it. But I'm not alone: a harbor seal is watching me. On its kelp-colored face is a look of concern; for what, I don't know, but it is an anxious look of concern. It catches my eye and slips out of sight.

That's about as much as I see of harbor seals on this excursion. Their distant relatives, California sea lions, are more visible. A herd advertises itself with much barking and waving of flippers. I can row to within a few feet of them, close enough to smell their fishy breath, before they take notice of me, roll their eyes, and dive. Harbor seals usually see me first, surfacing suddenly, and when I get too close, they don't dive—they just duck.

Not that much is known about harbor seals, although they inhabit coasts from Baja California to Japan and from New Jersey to Portugal. Without particular economic significance, they've been left alone compared to other marine "resources" like whales, sea otters, or fur seals. Enough inhabit the oceans to populate a medium-sized city, if the concept applied to them.

The Bay Area has one of the world's densest harbor seal populations, including a major breeding site, so one might think spying on them would be easy here, as with sea lions. But everything about harbor seals seems to work against that. Sea lions' glossy fur makes them glitter conspicuously in the water. Harbor seals' mottled gray-and-tan hair camouflages them. Sea lions are organized: huge crested males dominate females and young on breeding beaches. Harbor seals look alike, and although they are more social than they let on, they are discreet about it. Breeding congregations tend to be cryptic, and the seals seem to do little more than lie around together. Competition among males for females is not conspicuous, although individual squabbling is common enough.

Sizable harbor seal groups often bask on islands in the Bay, but it is not easy to distinguish them from rocks and sand because they lie around in a disorganized way. Sea lions usually bask with their heads toward the top of a reef, but harbor seals may be content to bask head down. It is easier to slip back into the water that way.

Much harbor seal private life goes on in the water and at night. Unlike sea lions, they can mate and give birth in the water. Somewhat paradoxically, considering how they love basking ashore, they can sleep in the water, surfacing to breath every ten minutes or so without awakening. They are generally more adapted to marine life than sea lions, which depend on their fur to keep warm, lacking the blubber layer that harbor seals have in common with whales. Sea lions move about fairly quickly on land because their hind legs turn forward and push them along. Seals have lost that ability.

All this suggests that seals' ancestors were in the sea longer than sea lions,' but the fossil record is inconclusive. Recognized sea lion ancestors have inhabited North America's Pacific coast for about 30 million years, whereas harbor seal ancestors may have appeared here much later. Their ancestors may have evolved elsewhere: there are fossils of harbor seal ancestors from the Atlantic, although they aren't older than the Pacific's sea lion ancestors. Paleontologists have found fossils of sea lion ancestors in the Bay Area, at Drakes Bay on Point Reyes, but they haven't found any such harbor seal fossils. Anyway, both the living genera probably are only a few million years old, not much older than the genus *Homo*.

Reference to human evolution, of course, brings up the question of intelligence, but harbor seals are no more confiding about this than about other parts of their lives. California sea lions clown in circuses and aquariums as "performing seals," but harbor seals are not so inclined. When researchers gave intelligence tests to both species, the results were strikingly divergent. Sea lions ran up impressive performance records, while harbor seal records were skimpy. Researchers complained of erratic response, of indifference to the rewards and deprivations that usually stimulate performance. From a behaviorist standpoint, such indifference might not suggest high intelligence. Still, the harbor seals did perform at times, so the researchers concluded that they were at least capable of learning—and very alert, since they spent a lot of time glancing around nervously.

A harbor seal's brain is larger and more convoluted than a dog's. Then why is it a bad student? Is intelligence a capacity to learn, or to be taught? Sea lion mothers nurture and instruct their land-born pups until they are ready to enter the water, and teaching continues within the herd at sea. Young sea lions congregate in "schools." Harbor seal mothers more or less abandon their pups after a three- to six-week nursing period, and the weaned pup gets no special treatment. The mother leaves it with a mantle of milk-fat, on which it lives until it starts to catch fish. Attrition of harbor seal pups is fairly high in the Bay Area's realm of great white sharks.

Still, there are plenty of seals: their range is expanding where humans don't persecute them. They seem to be born with survival skills, which would help explain a captive seal's indifference to a man with a stale herring in one hand and a clipboard in the other. It also might explain their lack of organization: seals don't seem to need each other as much as other brainy species do. Rich Schopen, a biologist at the Steinhart Aquarium in San Francisco who hand-raised two harbor seal pups, told me that a dolphin or orca would die if kept in a tank alone, but a harbor seal wouldn't.

One might conclude that harbor seals are poor company. On the contrary, individuals have become greatly attached to humans on occasion. In her book *Seal Morning*, Rowena Farr describes raising a harbor seal on the isolated Scottish coast. The seal, a female named Lora, preferred to sleep in the author's bed and developed a passion for musical instruments, including a harmonica, a xylophone, and a toy trumpet, on which she practiced every day and learned several tunes. Farr doesn't say she taught Lora any of this.

The environmental barriers between the human mind and that of marine mammals like harbor seals are profound. Seals inhabit a world that continually liberates tremendous amounts of energy. Boulders shake as waves pounds them; surf rips through tidal channels. Seals duck under beach breakers like human swimmers but move with ease in currents no human could withstand, the same currents that bring them their food.

They lead a double life between land, which may seem strangely ethereal to them, and sea, which must be unimaginably sensual. Bay Area seals inhabit the giant kelp forest, a match for tropical rain forest in its diversity of sights, smells, and sounds—especially sounds.

Harbor seals' apparent taciturnity is another of their equivocal qualities. Water carries aural vibrations much better than air, so seals' underwater hearing and vocalizations are complex. Rowena Farr writes: "Seals have perhaps the largest vocal range among mammals. Their repertoire includes grunts, snorts, barks, peculiar mewing hisses, and a wail which often rises from a deep base to a treble." Under water, they use a special range of clicking sounds that may allow them to echolocate, to "see" by hearing echoes as bats and whales do. They probably can hear tremendous distances, perhaps listening for the sounds of salmon and lampreys moving up rivers, or of orcas communicating with each other far out to sea.

Harbor seals' visual world may resemble humans' more than their aural one, but again it's hard to say. I got a close look at harbor seal eyes when Rich Schopen introduced me to his protégés at the Steinhart Aquarium, and they are strangely beautiful. The iris is an intricate zigzag pattern of gold, amber, and brown—like an abstract Rembrandt—and the pupil is an indescribable shape. It is hard to imagine how such eyes function, although they are set well forward in the head, suggesting good depth and distance perception. Their environment provides them with a lot to see anyway—in both air and water, day and night, vast sandy bottoms and intricate kelp forests.

Henry Wood Elliott, a nineteenth-century seal expert, wrote: "There are few eyes in the orbits of men and women which suggest more pleasantly the ancient thoughts of their being windows of the soul." Humans living near harbor seals have often associated them with passage into a spirit world. Some believed that seals could come ashore, take off their skins, and live for some time as humans. But that seems anthropocentric to me. With all the unfathomable qualities they have evolved, why would harbor seals want to do that?

—*Clear Creek*, May 1971

pelicans and pantyhose

Driving around Oakland's Lake Merritt is misleading. The lake seems raggedly artificial, a run-down vestige of genteel Victorian landscaping. The lake does have an artificial side. It originated in the 1860s when Samuel Merritt—an early land developer—dammed a polluted tidal inlet to make a setting for mansions like one he was building. Highrises and apartment houses of a certain Raymond Chandler ambience replaced the mansions, although the city turned part of the north shore into a park. Yet a walk around the lake will show that it is not just urban decoration. It is still a working part of San Francisco Bay's ecosystem, connected by a tidal channel to the San Leandro estuary. Bay waters still ebb and flow in it, albeit controlled by floodgates.

As I write, the first winter storms are passing through, bringing two phenomena that embody Lake Merritt's connection to the Bay. First, storm sewers drain the summer's accumulation of litter and grime into the lake, an extraordinary welter of plastic, paper, dead cats, torn underwear—everything imaginable—all filmed with an iridescent engine oil slick that swirls on the lake's surface. Tides flush some of this out into the Bay and ultimately into the ocean, although the city has to clean much of it. Second, the storms bring flocks of migratory and/or marine birds to the lake, where they feed and shelter for the winter: ducks, grebes, phalaropes, gulls, pelicans, coots, egrets, and cormorants, among others.

But what do the birds eat in this welter of garbage and muck? They eat the products of a rich, functioning ecosystem, albeit a dirty one.

A look into the lake reveals the basic elements. Mingled with Styrofoam cups and Big Mac containers are sheets and strands of algae, the photosynthetic producers at the food pyramid's base. During the warm seasons, algal blooms fill the lake, breeding disagreeable smells but also many small shrimp and other invertebrates. These feed small fish—mainly smelt and gobies—and they all reach astronomical numbers by October. A look into the lakeshore then will reveal smelt schools that shadow every inch of the bottom with their nervously darting bodies.

Algae, small invertebrates, and bacteria also feed large numbers of clams and mussels, and aquatic worms that live in white, limy cases and filter food from the water with bushy green gills. These organisms hide in the muck or attach to the lake's stone margins, beer cans, or any other convenient substrate. Dead ones' cases and shells cover the lake bottom.

In the fall, lowered temperatures and chemical changes in the water kill most of the algae, bringing famine and panic to swollen fish populations. Droves of small fish flee from larger ones into the shallows, where both become vulnerable to arriving birds. Sometimes schools suddenly die off, the bodies attracting large flocks of ring-billed and California gulls, which, lacking the skills of cormorants or diving ducks, ordinarily have to fish from the sidelines or rob other birds.

Lake Merritt's odd mix of urbanity and biotic productivity make it a good place to watch fishing birds. Gulls and egrets are so used to joggers and roller skaters that they ignore them whizzing past, although they fly away if I walk too near them. But if I'm discreet I can often watch the birds stalking and catching fish from a few feet away.

The bird assemblage this fall was spectacular. A flock of brown pelicans—a dozen adults and half again as many juveniles—fed in the inlet between Kaiser Center and Lakeside Park. They sat in the water with their beaks tucked against their breasts, then somehow knew that a fish school was nearby and took off together, an ungainly flapping that quickly turned to graceful soaring just above the surface. Spotting fish, they dived into the water and opened their bill pouches, so they seemed to have veined balloons attached to their chests, thus trapping many small victims to be swallowed once the pouch was raised out of the water.

I doubt that the pelicans located the fish schools themselves. They were just the most conspicuous predators on them. Bonaparte's gulls and Forster's terns seemed more likely fish-finders, since they fly higher and dive nimbly to catch fish in their sharp beaks. I saw a Bonaparte's gull dive into a foot of water below where I stood on the sidewalk and fly away with a several-inch-long goby I hadn't noticed. Or perhaps the cormorants, with their underwater swimming skills, were the fish-finders that the other birds watched.

Whatever its workings, the birds' feeding was definitely coordinated. When the pelicans, Bonaparte's gulls, and terns left one part of the inlet for another, they were soon followed by the snowy and common egrets and the California and ring-billed gulls that had loitered in the shallows hoping to catch something scared by them. They were like spectators in tennis whites following a water polo game from one end of a swimming pool to another, with the splashing and shrieking of a country club crowd.

Fall is the most active time on the lake. In winter, rafts of ducks stay on the sheltered east side, but they're quieter than the fall birds. They rest on the water with their beaks tucked under their wings. Equally idle cormorants often line the log boom that divides the ducks from the main part of the lake. But there's still a lot going on. When the floodgates at the lake's west end open to let in the tide, large fish appear in the current under the bridge. It's hard to identify them, but they include sharks and striped bass.

In spring most of the birds leave for cleaner spots. Some try to nest on little wooded islands offshore from the Rotary Nature Center at Lakeside Park, but a colony of night herons that also nests there makes this difficult. The water clears and gets less littered after the rains taper off and before the algal bloom gets under way. This is a good time to watch the lake's underwater doings, which can be as interesting as the birds' fishing, if less spectacular.

I was walking beside the lake one bright warm day last spring when I noticed small fish darting individually among the algal clots that were starting to form. They weren't smelt or gobies, so I stopped for a closer look and saw that some were a bright metallic blue, with ruby red bellies. They hovered over certain algae patches and chased away similar fish that approached. Sometimes they made quivering motions above the algae patches or burrowed into them.

I realized that they were male sticklebacks defending nest territories. Ethologists and biology teachers like sticklebacks because of their curious breeding habits. A male makes a nest in an algae patch by burrowing a tunnel. Then he lures cruising egg-laden females into it with a zigzag courtship dance. Once a female's in the nest, he encourages her with nudging motions to lay her eggs, fertilizes them, and then chases her away. He repairs the nest and starts dancing to attract females again until he has a satisfactory egg collection, which he incubates by standing on his head in front of the nest and fanning oxygenated water into the tunnel with his pectoral fins. When they hatch, he anxiously guards the tiny fry, keeping them in a tight school. If one wanders away, he darts after it, catches it in his mouth, and carefully spits it back into his school.

I'd never seen wild sticklebacks, and I hadn't expected to see them in downtown Oakland. Proceeding along the lakeshore, I saw bright blue males guarding algae patches every few feet—it was a stickleback city. I couldn't stand and watch the whole breeding process since joggers and roller skaters would have knocked me into the lake if I had tried, but I was able to see the progress of the nests over the next few weeks. By the end of June, the algae clots teemed with thousands of tiny sticklebacks that were well protected in their filmy green chambers. One such school hovered over an open copy of *Basic Math,* which some liberated student had flung into the lake. I imagined the tiny fish doing their sums, instructed by a small whitish crab that sidled over the mussel shells on which the textbook rested.

—*Berkeley Monthly*, February 1980

the living, dying bay

ADJECTIVES FOR A SUPERORGANISM

Crossing San Francisco Bay in an inflatable boat is surprising when you're used to crossing on bridges. It isn't simply that you see more of the Bay that way. You have to see more. Otherwise, the Bay will bounce you around. You learn to watch for waves that can fling loose objects skyward; in fact, you learn what it is to be such an object as your shoes say good-bye to the deck and your binoculars wind themselves around your neck. You find that the Bay is more than a stretch of water for building bridges over, that it has palpable rhythms and moods that make it (as far as you in your inflatable boat are concerned) alive.

I discovered these things one May morning as the guest of an excursion company, San Francisco Bay Adventures. We set out from Sausalito and ran up Richardson Bay off Marin County to the Audubon sanctuary there. Michael Herz, a senior research scientist at Tiburon's Center for Environmental Studies, wanted to look at a harbor seal gathering spot nearby. But new building apparently had scared off the seals, so we turned around and headed toward the Golden Gate. I wasn't too impressed with the Bay up to that point. Walled with condominiums and houseboats, it seemed inert and opaque.

The Bay corrected my impression south of Sausalito. Within a few yards, air and water changed from smoggy suburban to sparkling marine as we approached the Gate. The boat jounced through a line of waves that had me holding on to my notebook with my toes, then broke into a simmering turbulence like a gigantic whirlpool bath. Terns and pelicans didn't just fly over, they sailed. Looking eastward, I saw a broad stretch of white water, as though a school of fish or a rocky shoal were breaking the surface. Michael Herz said that the incoming and outgoing tides were meeting there, and he pointed out veins of foam that showed interfaces of salt- and freshwater. During winter floods, he added, river water roaring out of the Gate can move the interface with ocean water as far offshore as the Farallon Islands.

Even during normal outgoing tides, several times more water flows through the Golden Gate than through the Mississippi's mouth. The Bay's power and exuberance reminded me of gray whales I'd seen spouting at Half Moon Bay. In a sense, I was watching the Bay spout— breathe—as I watched the tides swirl past, because tides and rivers are what keep the Bay alive just as air keeps whales alive. Yet I still felt confused about the Bay's functioning. Big as whales are, they are easier to comprehend than a 435-square-mile bay. I didn't understand the sudden intensity of the change from Richardson Bay to the Golden Gate.

When I stopped at the Army Corps of Engineers' Bay Model in Sausalito on the way home, I began to understand. With its gray concrete surface and computerized voice ticking off the lunar days, the thirty-year-old model gives little sense of the Bay's vitality. It does give a very graphic sense of the contrast between most of the Bay's flat, shallow bottom and the huge underwater canyon that tides and floods have carved through the Golden Gate. Even in the model, where the canyon is three feet deep, its bottom is invisible. I was surprised to realize what an abyss I'd been floating, or rather bouncing, over.

Likening the Golden Gate to a gray whale's spout may seem farfetched, but many other analogies between the Bay and a living organism are possible. Like a gray whale, the Bay has a life span, an anatomy, and a physiology. It's just that they are so extended in time and space that we have trouble perceiving them.

THE AGING, RENEWING BAY

San Francisco Bay has existed for at least ten thousand years, since melting ice sheets flooded its basin by raising ocean levels. Because the basin has existed much longer, as sideways movements of the Pacific and North American tectonic plates cracked and tilted California into mountains and valleys, the Bay has had ancestors at various times during the past few million years. A new bay would form when ocean levels were high during interglacial periods, then gradually silt in and revert to land when ocean waters receded.

The rise of California's mountains did more than form the Bay's basin. The barrier of the Coast Range forced most of the state's main rivers to drain into the Pacific through the single outlet of the Golden Gate. Thus the Bay became not only an inland arm of the Pacific but a maritime extension of the Sacramento and San Joaquin river systems—a great estuary where most of the runoff from the Sierra Nevada and southern Cascades meets the ocean. Someday, the rivers will end this Bay's natural life span by filling it with silt and sand eroded from the mountains. It may already be half full of sediments. They lie three hundred feet deep in places, and average water depth is only twenty feet.

Ocean and rivers shape the Bay's anatomy. Sea level determines its extent, while rivers deposit marshy flats of silt and sand that divide open water from land. Tidal flows carve sloughs that carry water into brackish and salt marshes, while rivers and creeks cut deltaic channels and backwaters lined with freshwater marshes and riparian woodlands. Tides and streams together cut deep underwater channels that circulate throughout the Bay and converge eventually on the Gate.

Ocean and rivers regulate the Bay's physiology. Tides that move water in and out of marshes and mudflats twice a day bring food and oxygen to organisms and carry off waste. Rivers transport vast amounts of mineral and organic nutrients into the Bay to be cycled through wetlands, mudflats, and open waters. Storms can increase rivers' winter and spring flows sixfold. The Bay could no more stay alive without these circulating fluids than a gray whale could live without its blood. Fresh nutrients and water must continually replenish the Bay or it will be starved and poisoned. When upriver water users say that freshwater allowed to run through the Bay to the ocean is wasted, it makes as much biological sense as saying that a whale's blood is wasted in the whale.

Estuarine wetlands such as the Bay's are earth's most productive habitats, fabricating four times as much green plant matter from the raw materials of sunlight, water, and silt as agribusiness cornfields. Warm waters swarming with bacterial action quickly transfer nutrients from silt to photosynthetic cells, and burgeoning algae and marsh plants form primary links in thousands of food chains. Reduced by bacteria to protein-rich detritus, they nourish vast swarms of tiny animals that drift in and out of marshes with the tide, including the young of many larger species—crabs, shrimps, fish, worms, oysters, and clams. The small drifters feed masses of other slightly larger predators that inhabit the Bay or pass through it at some stage in their lives, as with salmon and striped bass. From there, food chains ramify in myriad directions that lead eventually to egrets, cormorants, pelicans, grebes, and diving ducks; to six Bay shark species, one of which may grow to over fifteen feet in length; to hundreds of other fish species; to harbor seals, sea lions, and gray whales.

The Bay is like an enormous turbine, spinning and generating energy as organisms feed, are fed upon, and pass their nutrients along. Far from dissipating this energy, the Bay recycles it with endless ingenuity. A carbon atom carried into the delta by the Sacramento or San Joaquin might make hundreds of passages through the turbine before escaping through the Gate. At first, the atom would ride above the tides flowing in through Carquinez Strait, since freshwater is lighter than salt. It might get pushed up a slough that feeds a delta marsh, enter the roots of a tule sedge, become part of a leaf's photosynthetic factory, then drift downstream to San Pablo Bay as detritus. There, a bay shrimp might ingest it or the tide might push it up another slough, into a salt marsh, where it would undergo the process of incorporation and decay in a pickleweed. Mixed with the Bay's saltier waters, it then might sink to the bottom to be consumed by a worm, then by a sand dab. It might stay on the sand through generations of bottom organisms and their predators before tidal flows move it again, and when they do, they might push it back up Suisun Bay instead of pulling it down the final rocky chute of the Golden Gate. Or it might stay in the Bay sediments, an organic speck in the silica matrix of future sandstone.

Understanding the Bay system's intricacies might require a brain as big as the Bay. But there is a more intuitive way of perceiving its vitality. Like a gray whale, the Bay is beautiful, and while this quality can't be experienced whole, except perhaps from an orbiting satellite, it can be in hundreds of parts: on a fall afternoon at China Camp State Park, when wooded islands float in a haze above salt marshes and thousands of blackbirds flock on the horizon . . . on a winter evening at San Pablo Bay National Wildlife Refuge, when hundreds of shorebirds rest on mudflats the color of the setting sun . . . on a spring morning at San Francisco Bay

National Wildlife Refuge, when orange parasitic plants called dodder growing on pickleweed glow like fire in the green matrix.

The Bay is beautiful—that is, where it is reasonably healthy, which raises another characteristic of living organisms. They can die from injury or disease as well as old age. San Francisco Bay has suffered more than its share of injury in the past two centuries, as silt from Mother Lode mining has smothered its bottom and landfill for urban growth has obliterated more than a third of its original acreage. Indeed, various growth schemes would have filled most of it if the Save the Bay movement hadn't begun in the 1960s. Jack Foster succeeded in dumping 1.5 million truckloads of rubble into the Bay to make Foster City in 1962. A decade later, David Rockefeller failed to cut off the top of San Bruno Mountain to make a Manhattan-sized Bay island.

Unfortunately, stopping the Bay's physical obliteration is not enough to save it. Growth has diseased as well as injured it by destroying more than 90 percent of its wetlands, diverting more than 60 percent of its river flows, decimating its biota, and contaminating waters, wetlands, and wildlife with sewage, refinery wastes, pesticide residues, and many other things—an alphabet soup of toxic elements, from arsenic to zinc.

None of the professional Bay-watchers (a research scientist, an environmentalist, a Coast Guard licensed operator, and a boating entrepreneur) who went with me on the inflatable excursion to the Golden Gate doubted for a minute that the Bay was sick and getting sicker. The licensed operator, salty-looking Captain Joshua Mills, saw some improvement in water quality from past decades, when "the water was so black in places you could drop a ham sandwich in it and even a gull wouldn't touch it." But he expressed amazement that the Bay had lasted as long as it had, given the pressures on it.

"Improved water quality won't help the Bay in the long run if all the habitat is lost to development," said environmentalist John Amodio of the Bay-Delta Preservation Trust.

"Cleaning up sewage and factory discharges won't even improve water quality if agribusiness keeps diverting more water," said scientist Michael Herz. "I wouldn't eat a striped bass out of the Bay now, even if the population wasn't down 80 percent from the 1960s."

"I'm afraid the Bay is finished as a commercial fishery," said recreation entrepreneur Jerry Cadagan, president of San Francisco Bay Adventures. "The San Joaquin River has become a toxic drain. And what's so frustrating about this is that further water diversion for irrigation isn't even going to help agribusiness in the long run. It's just letting them grow crops that are already in surplus while they poison their soil with salt and selenium."

"The Bay Area is supposed to be environmentally enlightened," said Amodio, "but there hasn't been a concerted effort to manage the Bay as an integrated ecosystem. Government bodies have concentrated on their own little fiefdoms, and the conservation community has been trapped responding to political fragmentation. They're doing better back east in places like Chesapeake Bay. They had a Year of the Bay there. When have we ever had a Year of the Bay? It's embarrassing."

"It's truly awesome just how much has been wrecked," said Joshua Mills. There wasn't much to say after that. We finished our sandwiches in the hot sun of a Sausalito deck restaurant and went home.

THE ENDANGERED, ETERNAL BAY

The Bay-watchers' words had the ring to truth, but, coming from four directions, they caused something of the confusion I'd felt at the Golden Gate. Threats to the Bay are numbingly diverse. I wondered if it might clarify things to consult some kind of human Bay Model, one individual with official authority, scientific knowledge, environmental concern, and practical day-to-day experience on the Bay. It sounded a little like Superman, but I headed to San Francisco Bay National Wildlife Refuge's new visitor center in Fremont to see what I could find.

I began to think I'd come to the right place when wildlife biologist Tom Harvey listed the things he dealt with on his job. I managed to scribble "water quality, salt ponds, seasonal wetlands, endangered species, diving ducks, colonial nesting birds, the Army Corps of Engineers, the Coast Guard, developers, conservation groups, the Leslie Salt Company, oil spills, wildlife disease epidemics" in my notebook, but others got past me.

"We're spread kind of thin here," said Harvey, a thirty-three-year-old with outdoorsy good looks. He'd had the job for five years but has lived near the Bay all his life. "My parents had a house on the estuary at Alameda," he said, "so the Bay was in the backyard. I remember as a kid being turned on by the richness of life just on a piling or under a rock."

When I asked him if he thought of the Bay as a living organism, Harvey hesitated, apparently a little surprised by the question. It did sound like deep ecology woo-woo philosophizing in the mundane context of the refuge headquarters' meeting room, with regulations manuals and memos on the bulletin board, and people in tan uniforms busy at desks next door.

"Yeah, I think I do," he finally said. "Particularly in the sense of trying to maintain it in a state of health. You have to consider the whole thing to do that.

"I didn't really start out seeing it that way. My degree is in ornithology, so originally I was just studying birds. When I got this job, there were so many outside influences on the Bay that I had to develop a sense of the whole. We can't just worry about what's inside the refuge boundaries or we'll lose that too, eventually."

I asked him if he thought the Bay was getting sicker. His response was unhesitating. "Absolutely. I've seen it become a less vital place just in my lifetime. The water quality picture is bleak, especially in the South Bay here. There just isn't enough water coming in to flush out the increasing contaminant levels from all the new development. It isn't just sewage and factory wastes. A lot of it is grease and oil washing off roads into storm drains.

"We're still losing habitat that refuge wildlife needs. When it was established in the early 1970s, the planners concentrated on saving the mudflats, salt marshes, and salt ponds because those were considered the sensitive areas, the ones the waterfowl, shorebirds, shellfish, and endangered species needed. Now we're finding that seasonal marshes inshore from the tidal areas are important too. We used to think the salt marsh harvest mouse [a federally endangered species] was mostly in the tidal marshes, but we've discovered that the largest populations are in the seasonal marshes, and the seasonal marshes are going under to development. We're protecting one part of the Bay and letting another deteriorate. It's like somebody quitting smoking but taking snuff."

I knew what Harvey meant by growth pressures. When I'd started going to places like Coyote Hills Regional Park in the early 1970s, much of the South Bay had been in open fields inhabited by ring-necked pheasants and burrowing owls. Driving to my interview with Harvey, I'd passed exactly two open spaces, one with a big Realtor's sign on it, the other part of the Ardenwood Technology Park, which proclaimed its presence with an outdoor fountain and floral display. The fountain seemed ironic in light of Harvey's talk of water scarcity, throwing gallons into the air beside a freeway where gridlocked commuters were unlikely to enjoy it.

"The freshwater input from the delta is really critical," Harvey continued, "particularly down here where the pollution concentrates. If we lose more of that . . . It's hard not to pessimistic."

Harvey hesitated again when I asked him if he thought the Bay would survive. It's the kind of anthropomorphic question that scientists, especially government ones, may not like, but Harvey did his best to answer it.

"There'll be some kind of bay here. In fact, the Bay will probably grow in the next century because the greenhouse effect is expected to raise ocean levels. It will flood a lot of the present wetlands, so if we don't save more open space around the Bay now, there may not be any wetlands in the future, just open water next to houses and factories. That will mean even less wildlife. If river inflow keeps decreasing, the Bay will become more of a marine environment—that is, if increased contamination doesn't cause some truly awesome disaster.

"The threats to the refuge are so diverse that there's a temptation to get cynical, to say, 'This place is dying: who cares. I'll go to Alaska or Oregon.' But then you go out in the field and see something that reminds you why you keep wading through the paperwork and the meetings. A while ago I was in Richmond looking for California clapper rails [another endangered species]. After three days, I finally found a nest in an area that stank of oil refineries, was covered with landfills and junkyards, and had packs of dogs roaming around. All signs of the high value we've placed on wetlands. But then there was this beautiful bird nesting in the middle of this stuff. I was struck by the tenacity. It was sad. But it was a testimonial to something."

I walked around the visitor center's nature trail after talking to Harvey. Salt ponds separated the trail from the Bay, and it seemed another irony that we consider them wildlife habitat now, since they replaced natural marshes and were used to produce industrial chemicals. Still, there was wildlife. Black-necked stilts waded daintily in the brine, probing with their slightly upturned bills and complaining raucously as I approached. Swallows skimmed around nests on an old duck-hunting shack. When I stopped to examine some unpleasant-looking blotches in the ponds, I saw that even they were alive, containing thousands of tiny red brine shrimp.

THE WALLED-IN, UNTAMABLE BAY

It was clear from what Tom Harvey had said that the less urbanized North Bay and delta are crucial to the Bay-as-organism, so I headed in that direction one hot, smoggy October day. I'd long wanted to see Suisun Marsh, the largest single estuarine marsh in the continental United States, but somehow never had, despite driving past it many times on I-80. The sprawl around Fairfield hadn't promised much in the way of open space.

I got a pleasant surprise after negotiating the raw housing tracts and malls around Suisun City. From Peytonia Slough Ecological Reserve at its northern end, Suisun Marsh stretched south toward the Contra Costa hills, with only a solitary barge crane to hint at industrial activity. It was about as close as I'd come to seeing California lowland in a truly wild state, a sweep of tule rushes, cattails, sedges, and wild grasses extending to the horizon. Asters and marsh grindelia added blue, white, and yellow to the marsh plants' bright green. White-crowned sparrows whistled, marsh wrens chattered, a loggerhead shrike rasped, and an unseen bird, perhaps one of Tom Harvey's rails, clucked from the tule sedges.

I was even more surprised when a river otter surfaced in the slough. I'd never seen one so close to a town. It stuck its nose in the air and chewed on a small fish like a dog enjoying a succulent bone. When it saw me, it dove and resurfaced behind a clump of rushes, but it wasn't really alarmed, and I watched it eat two more fish, turning on its back to chew them corncob style. Sweltering in the 90-degree, hydrocarbon-laced air, I envied it.

When I drove southeast to Grizzly Island, I found more open spaces. Early-arriving migratory waterfowl dotted ponds, and the brushy levees and roadsides at the state wildlife area produced many squawking cock pheasants. Two black-shouldered kites, showy white raptors that specialize in marshy, grassy terrain, watched me from a coyote bush, flying away only when I was a few yards from them.

Yet there was a difference between Grizzly Island and the Peytonia Reserve that implied some doubts about the future health of marsh and delta. Although by no means pristine (much of Suisun Marsh was drained and farmed in the 1920s and '30s), the marsh around Peytonia Reserve is natural, maintained by the interaction of river flows and tidal action that has regulated Bay wetlands for millennia. What I saw of Grizzly Island, on the other hand, is heavily managed for agriculture or to produce game and fish for sport consumption. Rather than allowing wetlands to operate according to a natural water regimen, managers flood or drain the land to optimize crop or game production. The state wildlife area is plowed and bulldozed into squares that might as well be farm fields, except that they aren't (I hope) laced with pesticides.

There's nothing wrong with managing duck habitat, especially at a time when waterfowl populations are dwindling alarmingly, but increased emphasis on artificial management showed its ominous side as I talked to people concerned about the future. Under current policies, only diked marshes managed by hunting clubs or the state are assured of dependable freshwater supplies. As more water is diverted from the delta, saltwater creeps into the natural, open marshes. Brackish marshes of rushes and brass buttons turn into salt marshes of pickleweed and cordgrass, habitats less favorable to many wildlife species. Eventually, such places may become so salty as to be almost sterilized.

The state Department of Water Resources proposes various engineering solutions to salt intrusion, such as the massive dam and floodgates it is building near the mouth of Montezuma Slough, Suisun Marsh's main source of Sacramento River water. The gates are supposed to let freshwater into the marsh and keep saltwater out. But an environmentalist I talked to, Bay Institute founder Bill Davoren, likened such engineering solutions to putting Band-Aids on a failing kidney. Like kidneys, brackish marshes filter pollutants and toxins out of water that ends up in faucets as well as in wildlife habitat. If the 85,500-acre "kidney" of Suisun Marsh should fail, it's hard to imagine a dialysis that could replace its filtering function in any permanent way.

After leaving Grizzly Island, I went to the Sacramento River at Rio Vista, heading east on Route 12 over miles of parched rangeland that seemed as unlike Suisun Marsh as the Kansas Plains. The river looked like a lot of water by the time I reached it. But appearances can be deceptive. In the drought year of 1931, delta water got so salty that residents couldn't drink it or irrigate with it. River flow had become so low that saltwater had moved upstream to replace it. Freshwater flow acts as a barrier to saltwater intrusion, the only one that has proven effective.

Driving along the Sacramento's levee was more comfortable than crossing the Golden Gate in an inflatable boat. Yet, even walled behind levees, the river had a slightly disturbing grandeur that recalled the Gate's powerful tidal surge. This has to do with the fact that the river's surface is higher than the fields and orchards bordering it. Peaty delta soils subside when drained for agriculture, while sedimentation raises the levee-contained riverbed's level above the surrounding land. Engineers say the river is "tamed," but "caged" might be a better adjective. If it gets out of the levees, it won't be tame.

River and Golden Gate both had an incalculable look, perhaps because they are the Bay's main links with the biosphere. The rivers link it to the mountains; the Gate to the ocean. Looking into the Sacramento's swift flow, I didn't feel that I understood much of what was going on down there, for all the paper and talk I'd waded through. I didn't know as much as the big chinook salmon that were cruising off the Gate. They'd know from the river's taste or smell when the Sacramento was right for them to swim up to spawn, and some would manage it despite everything civilization has put in their way: gill nets, salt intrusion, aqueduct pumping stations, dams, log jams, silted spawning streams. A lot fewer manage it now than even a few years ago, but somehow some still do. My facts and figures seemed thin compared to their knowledge.

Sometimes it seems that our ignorance makes a mockery of even our well-meaning attempts to protect the Bay. Its life can be frustratingly indifferent to our concern, as with Tom Harvey's clapper rail nesting in a landfill instead of the refuges we've made for it. But people keep trying, driven by that "something" Harvey mentioned. It might be a clapper rail or a salmon run or a day's sailing inside the Gate, but I think it amounts in the end to a recognition that the Bay's health reflects our own, that we can't draw a line between living integrity and mere exploitable matter without sooner or later finding ourselves on the wrong side of the line.

—*Image* magazine, *San Francisco Examiner*, December 6, 1987

the crowded desert islands

One of my adolescent fantasies was of a desert island, a small one with just a cliff and a beach. I'd live in a cave in the cliff and comb the beach. I had it on Sunday nights, before I had to go back for another week of junior high school, thus its appeal. This became less urgent as I got older, but I still liked the idea. When I came to California, I thought about such a place. Robert Louis Stevenson's *Treasure Island* is supposed to be based on the California coast.

Living around San Francisco Bay, I developed a mild fixation on the Farallones, a 221-acre island cluster twenty-seven miles off the Golden Gate. I'd see them on clear days as I hiked a ridge at Point Reyes, sugar-loaf shapes jutting from an otherwise empty ocean, and feel a faint frustration at their distance. They're an extension of the mainland, granite ridges dragged north from California's Transverse Ranges by tectonic plates, but the cold, windy Pacific cuts them off.

I first came to California to visit a friend who had a salmon fishing boat, at Bodega Bay. When I arrived the boat was broken, and all I ever got to do was help him unsuccessfully try to fix it. The farthest out I got was on a rowboat on Tomales Bay, east of Point Reyes. The Farallones just hovered out there. Tectonic plates might have dragged them north to the Aleutians—as they eventually will—so far as I was concerned.

I finally got to visit the Farallones years later when an Oceanic Society guide who was taking a writing course I taught at UC–Berkeley Extension gave me a free ride on a whale-watching trip there. The trip was not much like my solitary beachcombing fantasy. Few experiences are less solitary than a whale-watching cruise, and we didn't set foot on the islands, a national wildlife refuge reserved for breeding marine life. Yet those desert islands proved more fantastic—in the sense of diverse, surprising, curious, lively—than the fantasy one.

A half hour outside the Golden Gate, somebody said, "Look at the jellyfish." I glanced over the rail, expecting to see some of the little moon jellies and blue sailors that often wash ashore. A few drifted here and there, but below them floated an almost solid mass of golden brown, furry-textured disks, each as large as a child. They were close enough to the surface to see in detail but deep enough to appear shadowy and mysterious, and they extended in all directions—a mermaid's meadow of giant, pelagic chrysanthemums.

My student, Mike Ezekiel, said they were lion's mane jellyfish, each furry disk a colony of tiny coelenterates that strain microscopic plants and animals from the water with structures like miniscule poison darts on trailing filaments. I'd heard a lot about how fertile California's offshore waters are because of nutrient upwellings from deep currents, but I'd never seen such graphic evidence of it. The big jellyfish had to be floating in a plankton soup to be so abundant.

Many things we passed were new to me, although I'd been living a few miles from them for years. I didn't recall seeing the shy little harbor porpoises that showed dorsal fins for an instant as they surfaced to breathe. I'd seen a lot of penguin-like common murres on shoreline rocks, but I was unfamiliar with the pigeon guillemots that flew out of the boat's way, the little Cassin's auklets that dove out of its way, and the tufted puffins (named for the peroxide blond wings they seem to be wearing) that floated past. I'd seen red-necked phalaropes, but I hadn't seen those delicate shorebirds sitting on the deep-sea swells like gulls. Ezekiel said phalaropes like to follow blue whales and eat the shrimplike krill the whales feed on. They'd seen blues—the biggest animals that have ever lived—around the islands the day before.

We didn't see blue whales that day, but as we neared the main island we saw spouts and then flukes. A pod of gray whales was feeding in the shallows, sucking up bottom mud and straining out copepods and other small animals with the sieve-like baleen in their mouths. Of course, we couldn't see them doing this, just their tails as they dived and their mouths as they surfaced. Despite their semiconcealment, the gray whales' pale, mottled bodies had a weighty solidity, surprising in a medium that so far had mostly revealed amorphous jellyfish and kelp.

Even the best photographs can't convey this solidity: it must be seen in the flesh. It impressed the whale watchers so much that they cheered each time one surfaced.

As we passed the whales, something even stranger than lion's mane jellyfish appeared in front of the boat—a large circular object with one black eye, like a giant, animated tea tray out of *Through the Looking Glass*. When the prow neared it, the tray brandished stubby fins and upended itself, than shook a stubby tale and swam down out of sight. It was an ocean sunfish, or mola, a several-hundred-pound species that likes to sunbathe lying on its side on the surface. Mike Ezekiel had described it in one of his class essays, but I had assumed something so exotic lived only in the tropics. They come north to California's coast to eat the abundant jellyfish, although nobody knows how they get much nourishment from the watery coelenterates.

We steered past the island into deeper waters to look for more whales, and we soon found some humpbacks, a more pelagic species. Although larger than the grays, they seemed less substantial, more part of the amorphous marine world. Their dark, slick backs were hard to discern from the shifting swells, and they kept farther from the boat. They soon disappeared, probably diving to find plankton swarms.

A swarm of seabirds rested on the water, a sign of schooling fish, and we headed that way. A herd of California sea lions appeared, also headed for the fish. I hadn't seen sea lions swimming in a herd since a rowboat excursion when they'd startled me by rearing up out of the water exactly at sunset and barking in unison. Unlike the preoccupied whales, the lions craned their necks to eye us curiously. Some swam under the hull and appeared on the other side. One group hung back timidly, probably juveniles still getting used to things.

The lions departed as we turned back toward the islands, but a pod of black-and-white Dall's porpoises began to ride the boat's bow wave. A porpoise would surface just under the rail, glide effortlessly as the wave pulled it along, and then veer off to be replaced by another. "It's like they're doing it to be friendly," someone cried, although to me it seemed more like the daredevil exuberance of skateboarders attaching to cars.

As we approached Southeast Island, a fishy, ammoniac reek and a screeching din filled the air, then clouds of big black kelp flies that somehow managed to swarm around our heads despite the sea wind. The reason for all this soon became visible. Marine birds and mammals covered the island except for the empty buildings of a former lighthouse station. Gulls, murres, and cormorants sprinkled the tan granite like salt and pepper: their winged comings and goings blurred the horizon. When I focused my binoculars on what seemed to be blackish-brown moss on the seaside rocks, it resolved into masses of California sea lions, broken here and there with light brown patches of larger Steller's sea lions.

A litter of silvery, cylindrical objects covered one cove—basking elephant seals. They were so much larger than the sea lions that they confused my sense of scale. I thought of the first elephant seal I'd seen, a twenty-foot bull protruding from both ends of a willow thicket at Año Nuevo Rookery south of San Francisco like something back-projected in a monster movie. Once considered extinct, elephant seals have taken full advantage of protected rookeries since I first came to California in the late 1960s. Hundreds of bulls now rampage like blubbery buses up and down beaches. Away from rookeries, they live like sperm whales, swimming to mid-ocean and diving a mile deep to feed on abyssal squid and fishes.

The crowded desert islands were exciting, but they dispelled my adolescent fantasies of living on one. I felt no wish to land on the beach where the elephant seals sprawled. They've been known to run over unwary visitors. I felt even less wish to penetrate an island interior swarming with kelp flies, maggot-ridden guano, and territorial gulls. Wardens and scientific researchers need protective clothing to walk there.

The island may have been more pleasant during the nineteenth century, when commercial egg hunters and sealers had reduced their breeding populations to a fraction of today's restored ones. But I liked it the way it was. Thoreau wrote: We need to have some life "pasturing freely where we never wander." I think we also need to have some life rampaging, shrieking, and stinking freely where we never wander.

It was getting late, and the boat turned back. It had been a perfect August day, with a quiet sea and only a light fog. If we'd come out a few weeks later, when the fall storms had begun, things might have been less serene. Entire boatloads of whale watchers have succumbed to seasickness on blustery days. The islands' fauna also gets more active, as dozens of limousine-sized great white sharks arrive to feed on the seal population. Whale watchers sometimes see sharks decapitate unlucky seals and fling their bleeding bodies about. A few times, they have seen truck-sized orcas seize unlucky sharks and fling *their* bleeding bodies about.

I thought I'd seen almost everything for that time of year. As we plowed back into the lion's mane jellyfish pasture, however, Mike Ezekiel shouted, "A turtle!" A dark, spherical head and part of a ridged carapace protruded from the water a few yards off the bow. It was a leatherback, the largest sea turtle species: this one was at least five feet long. They appear around the Farallones occasionally, probably to graze on jellyfish. Leatherbacks are less confined to tropical waters than other species because their bulk minimizes heat loss.

I was still surprised to see a sea turtle in the chill waters off the Golden Gate. I was equally surprised to see another leatherback fifteen minutes later, long enough to be sure it wasn't the first. We got close enough to hear it breathing and to see limpets and barnacles on its carapace. Both turtles had orange patches on their heads and pinkish ones on their throats, colors I hadn't expected, possibly epiphytic organisms like the limpets and barnacles.

The turtles reminded me of one of my favorite childhood books, Time/Life's *The World We Live In*. It contains a painting of Mesozoic-era sea life, with plesiosaurs, ichthyosaurs, and mosasaurs swimming in an aquamarine ocean off a mountainous, palm-fringed coast. Those toothy reptiles were thrilling, but what most struck me was an enormous, leathery-shelled turtle swimming under them. It seemed a connection to my world as well as the distantly past one. "Why turtles were selected for survival on land and sea remains one of evolution's mysteries," the book said. That was in 1955, but it's still a mystery. But the fact that some sea turtles nest on desert islands probably contributes to it.

—*Manoa: A Pacific Journal of International Writing*, Winter 1993

a stop on the flyway

Oakland's Lake Merritt is, oddly enough, the oldest migratory bird refuge in the United States, established by the state in 1870 as a sanctuary for wintering ducks and other waterbirds. This was mainly for the benefit of the nouveau riche residents of mansions that ringed the lake after entrepreneur Samuel Merritt created it by damming a polluted tidal inlet to flush out the sewage. The residents probably liked having ducks to admire at the ends of their lawns: they certainly didn't want shotguns blasting away at them where their children and dogs were playing. Still, the little lake protected waterfowl during times when hunters thought nothing of killing hundreds a day, and it later played a surprising role in migratory bird science.

Bird migration is one of the great challenges to human understanding. Early records like the Bible mention it, but the "why," "how," and "where" of it remained mysteries. Classical Greek philosophers knew more about math and physics. Aristotle thought redstarts, summer migrants in Europe, turned into redbreasts in winter. (Old World redstarts and redbreasts are songbirds that resemble New World bluebirds, although they aren't blue.) The notion seems fanciful, but it was probably based on observation. Birds molt and change plumage before migrating, and species can be hard to distinguish then. Redstarts and redbreasts look similar anyway, so when redbreasts were present in winter, it made sense to see them as winter versions of redstarts. The redstart's winter home in Africa was unknown.

Two millennia later, the English essayist Robert Burton was as puzzled as the Greeks: "In winter not a bird is in Muskovy to be found," he writes in his 1621 *Anatomy of Melancholy,*

> but at the spring in an instant the woods and hedges are full of them, saith Herbastein. How comes it to pass? Do they sleep in winter like Gesner's Alpine mice; or do they lie hid, as Olaus affirms, in the bottoms of lakes and rivers, holding their breath? . . . Or do they follow the sun, as Peter Martyr manifestly convicts out of his own knowledge; for when he was ambassador in Egypt, he saw swallows, Spanish kites, and many such European birds in December and January. . . . Or do they lie hid in caves, rocks and hollow trees, as most think, in deep tin mines or sea cliffs, as Mr. Carew gives out?

Burton retained something of the medieval tradition of relying more on scholarship than personal observation for information. But two centuries later, Gilbert White, a close observer whose *The Natural History of Selborne* initiated today's nature writing tradition, remained unsure about many birds' seasonal disappearances from the Hampshire countryside, which he had studied all his life. Geographic exploration had shown that birds departing in the fall went south and that others came from farther north at the same time. But White still found it hard to believe that little finches, thrushes, and flycatchers could fly all the way to Africa. He also could not confidently reject the traditional belief that swallows and swifts dived into lakes and ponds to spend the winter dormant in mud. Their behavior contributed to this idea, since they spend a lot of time swooping over water to catch insects.

Technology solved those problems. Researchers put radio transmitters on white-fronted geese in California, follow them to Yukon Delta breeding grounds, then to wintering grounds in northwestern Mexico. But the "why" and "how" of migration remain problematic. We know that billions of birds move out of the tropics every spring, seeking the vast food and space resources of northern summer. We know almost nothing about the phenomenon's evolution.

Ornithologists once thought, for example, that showy songbirds like the orioles, tanagers, buntings, and warblers that nest here in summer evolved in North America and started migrating to the tropics when ice age cooling forced them south. But studies in the tropics found many resident species of our gaudiest summer migrants—orioles, tanagers, and buntings—and many are gaudier than ours. While some wood warbler species probably started migrating south because of global cooling, most of our summer songbirds probably moved north from the tropics as climate warmed. Two wood warbler species, the yellow-rumped and Townsend's, winter here, but the orioles, tanagers, and buntings all go south.

Each avian group has evolved its migration patterns differently, and fragile-boned birds leave few fossils. There are, fortunately, still plenty of living ones to study. Yet the results are bewilderingly complex. Various birds seem to use every migration method imaginable short of compass and sextant. Almost all migrants probably steer by coastlines, mountain ranges, and other landmarks to some degree. Social birds such as geese and cranes have traditional routes that they teach their young. On the other hand, many fledgling birds make their first migration independently, implying a genetic programming that prompts them to fly in the right direction for the right distance. (Sometimes they fly in the wrong direction, which is why the Bay Area regularly gets a few eastern or Old World birds.)

Night-flying migrants, of which there are many, may steer by the stars; day-flying ones by the sun or, on cloudy days, by polarized sunlight. Pigeons and doves have tiny deposits of magnetic crystals in their heads that allow them to orient themselves by earth's magnetic field. Some birds may hear low-frequency sounds like surf over long distances, which could help them follow coastlines or make landfalls when they are flying at twenty thousand feet at night, as many do.

Migratory birds have been a spectacular aspect of American history since Europeans arrived, if a sad one. Colonial naturalists, used to decimated Old World faunas, couldn't believe the abundance and diversity of the birds they found in eastern forests and wetlands, but it took only a few centuries to make those qualities, in fact, unbelievable. It is hard now to imagine eastern forests with clouds of passenger pigeons and flocks of Carolina parakeets. Avian faunas were less spectacular as the frontier moved through the arid West, but when Europeans reached the Bay Area, they found huge migratory bird concentrations. Sir Francis Drake provisioned his ship for crossing the Pacific with seabirds and mammals from the Farallon Islands.

As elsewhere, colonists quickly reduced those concentrations. Market hunting became a ruthlessly efficient industry and remained so into the early twentieth century. By the 1820s, Russian fur traders were killing fifty thousand western gulls a year on Farallon breeding islands for meat and feathers. Even the fishy-tasting eggs of seabirds such as murres from the Farallones became a profitable commodity in the days before chicken farms. An estimated four hundred thousand common murres originally nested on the islands; by 1900, "egging" had reduced the population to about twenty thousand.

In the long run, however, conversion of habitat, particularly Bay marshes, into farmland, salt ponds, and towns had a greater overall impact. It's hard to say what bird species habitat loss may have extirpated from the area, since little is known about what was here and the loss happened so fast. At least one disappearance is well-known, that of the yellow-billed cuckoo, a South American migrant that bred in Bay Area riparian woodlands into the nineteenth century. Civilization's thirst for irrigation water had expunged it by the twentieth.

Considering San Francisco Bay's importance as one of the world's major estuarine harbors, the late-nineteenth-century's conservation movement might have championed its bird habitats, but the Bay's economic potential outweighed this. John Muir may have worried about ducks and shorebirds as he managed his fruit ranch in Martinez in the 1880s and '90s, but there wasn't much he could do about Bay wetlands, as opposed to remote Yosemite. (And the city even got part of that in Hetch Hetchy Reservoir.) In 1909, the United States designated some of the Farallon Islands as a national wildlife refuge, but aside from kicking out the market hunters, it did little to protect wildlife. Through the 1920s, as early federal refuges dotted more rural regions, the Bay Area maintained the boomer stance typical of the forty-niner past. Entrepreneurs had plans for the Bay itself—filling it for real estate—and its waterfowl habitat didn't get even a nominal national refuge like the Farallones.

In the 1930s, a series of disastrous drought years coupled with the Depression focused attention on the need to protect some habitat for plunging bird populations and on opportunities to do so as land values also plunged. The federal government suddenly wanted more information about migrating birds—particularly the waterfowl that hunters value—and some kind of context for their overall management and protection. As it happened, little Lake Merritt—less posh by then after the mansion owners moved on but still offering winter refuge to water-fowl—played a big part in the enterprise.

An ornithologist named Frederick C. Lincoln had been running the U.S. Biological Survey since 1920. (The survey, a Department of Agriculture agency until its transfer to the Department of Interior in 1939, became the U.S. Fish and Wildlife Service, which runs today's refuges.) While accumulating banding and recovery records from across the continent, Lincoln had noted the faithfulness with which ducks and geese returned to the places where they'd been banded. Among pintails and widgeons banded at Lake Merritt from 1926 into the mid-1930s, he found that nearly 97 percent of band recoveries were made west of the Rockies. In the winter of 1933–1934, more than half the ducks trapped on the lake bore bands attached there in previous years.

There was a good evolutionary reason for this. Before its conversion into urban scenery, the tidal inlet that is now Lake Merritt had been ringed by extensive seasonal wetlands. The ducks banded there must have had ancestors that frequented the area going back many thousands of years. It is encouraging, in a way, that their ancestral wetland's conversion first to a sewer and then to a still-polluted ornamental lake didn't deter them from returning, although, given the overall situation, where else could they go?

Lincoln coordinated this data with material from other sites showing that different migrants, like shorebirds and songbirds, also often returned to the same nesting and wintering locations. He used the information to formulate the concept of the "flyway," a kind of avian nation "in which related migration routes . . . the lanes of individual travel from a particular breeding ground to the winter quarters of the birds that use them . . . are associated and blended in a definite geographical region."

Lincoln designated four North American flyways—the Atlantic, Mississippi, Central, and Pacific. They were shaped like tornadoes, wide in the boreal and arctic areas where many migratory waterbirds nest, then narrowing into migration routes through the United States, Mexico, and areas south. (Most North American migrants winter in Central America and the Caribbean, although some reach South America and a few, like Swainson's hawks, fly all the way to Patagonia.) Lincoln acknowledged that there was a lot of crossing from flyway to flyway, but aside from their soft edges, he considered them real biological entities. After World

War II the new Fish and Wildlife Service came to regard them as such, making them the basic administrative units for hunting regulations and refuge management.

Lincoln's work definitely contributed to migratory bird management. Since his death in 1960, however, ornithologists have largely discarded flyways as biological entities. One biologist who studies songbirds gave them a scathing review, calling them "misleading . . . hopeless, bogus . . . like saying the earth is flat . . . a disservice to science."

"Small birds are broad front migrants," he said. "They inherit an ability to fly a certain distance in a certain direction, and they don't care if there's an ocean or a mountain range in the way. Where's the flyway in that?" He grudgingly granted flyways limited usefulness for counting and managing geese, swans, and cranes but doubted their value for ducks, which he said fly in inherited directions and may change breeding grounds when following new yearly mating partners.

Most ornithologists agreed in milder terms, acknowledging flyways' significance as an administrative tool for managing species that follow strongly established migration routes. In his authoritative *Ducks, Geese, and Swans of North America*, Frank C. Bellrose called them "useful geographic terms . . . and political units" and cited some cases in which waterfowl migration "fit neatly into a flyway." But: "Flyways fail to define the passage of waterfowl because they cover too extensive an area and do not delineate movements of waterfowl that are lateral to a north-south direction."

Some avian groups, including most of the Bay Area's seabirds, definitely transgress the flyway concept. Brown pelicans nest on islands off southern California, then wander up and down the coast looking for food. White pelicans nest on inland lakes, then move to the coast for food. Some gull and tern species also go east to lake breeding grounds after wintering here. Other gulls and terns nest here, while some winter here and then fly north to breeding grounds. Common murres and pigeon guillemots that nest here may fly north for the winter as well as south. The notoriously endangered marbled murrelet spends winters feeding at sea and summers nesting in redwoods or Douglas firs.

Even with conventional migrants, flyways are more about administration than conservation: it's the ground and water where birds breed and feed that need to be protected, not the air they fly through. Lincoln wouldn't find much banding information on pintails and widgeons at

Lake Merritt these days. In his time, and until the early 1960s, several thousand of these dabbling ducks visited the lake in the fall. A few dozen visit it now, because there are a lot fewer ducks. Most migratory bird populations have declined steadily as habitat has disappeared.

Yet the federal government did little for Bay Area migratory bird habitat until the environmentalist uprising of Earth Day, 1970. The first federal refuge on the Bay came in 1972—Don Edwards San Francisco Bay National Wildlife Refuge, named for the congressman who helped push it past the growth boomers and through the legislature. San Pablo Bay NWR followed in 1974, through a similar process. (The Fish and Wildlife Service finally replaced the Coast Guard at Farallon NWR that year.) In 1980 the Bay Area got the only federal refuge established to protect endangered plants, Antioch Dunes NWR. A refuge established in 1992, 339-acre Marin Islands, protects the largest heron and egret rookeries in the Bay Area, although most of its acreage is under water.

Together, the four refuges on the Bay itself add up to somewhat more than fifty thousand acres of wetlands and other habitat. This protection represents massive efforts on the part of the local public. When Congress established San Pablo Bay NWR, for example, it comprised 175 acres, and local government had approved a 1,585-acre commercial and residential development nearby. One of the reasons for establishing the refuge was that 80 percent of the canvasback ducks in the Pacific Flyway were known to feed and rest on San Pablo Bay wetlands. Thousands of houses, apartments, and office buildings obviously would have impacted that. Citizens took government to court to force an environmental review and—with the help of then congressional representative Barbara Boxer and the U.S. Land and Water Conservation fund—finally saved the 1,585 acres by buying the land from a Japanese corporation for $7 million.

Yet the refuges don't represent a massive area considering that hundreds of thousands of wetland acres disappear from the continental United States every year. Of course, state, regional, and local parks also protect Bay Area wetlands, and conservationists led by David Brower, Edgar Wayburn, and Congressman Phillip Burton saved much migratory bird habitat when they pushed the United States to establish Point Reyes National Seashore and Golden Gate National Recreation Area. The restored marshes and riparian woodlands there are a revelation. But, considering the Bay's international significance as a unique ecological system (UNESCO designated it a biosphere reserve in 1988), one might think that the world's richest nation could do more.

Whatever the biological significance of Lincoln's avian nations, it's hard to get much sense of the Bay as more than a "stop on the flyway" from the National Fish and Wildlife Service refuges here. In the Central Valley refuges, the surrounding farmland's open horizon gives a certain feeling of integrity, albeit a truncated one. The Bay Area's refuges can seem like museums because the surrounding artificial environment is so pervasive.

When I visited San Pablo Bay one late spring day in 2014, the lone hiking trail to the marshes at Lower Tubbs Island led past huge hay fields and spoil banks for most of its length. At Tubbs Island, the trail became impassible because a stretch had collapsed into the marsh and the NFWS lacked the money to fix it. This being the off-season, water-birds were scarce anyway, aside from a few mallards and egrets. As I walked out to where the trail had collapsed, a buzzing roar like a swarm of giant insects erupted from the north. Looking that way, I saw dark objects zipping up a hillside like giant bees scurrying around a hive. It was like a 1950s atomic mutant movie. Then I remembered— it was the Sears Point Raceway.

The South Bay around Don Edwards Refuge is more urbanized than San Pablo Bay, but its marshes seem less constricted because more public facilities exist. When I walked the trails around the visitor center a few days after my San Pablo hike, the warehouses, hotels, and tech-nology parks to the east seemed to fade on the horizon, although they'd looked real enough as I drove in (albeit with surprising numbers of empty parking lots and FOR LEASE signs). I saw more birds than at San Pablo—shoveler ducks as well as mallards, gulls dipping into salt ponds, swallows nesting on an old hunting shack—but the only spectac-ular sight was a flock of white pelicans, and they weren't flying over the refuge but over Coyote Hills Regional Park to the north.

A wildlife kiosk on one of the restored Don Edwards marshes referred tersely to the flyway concept: "On the west coast, most birds migrate between their summer and winter homes along a migration corridor known as the Pacific Flyway." A kiosk on the impassible trailhead at the San Pablo Refuge reflected the concept's present status more appo-sitely. One panel had a block of biological boilerplate about the flyway superimposed on a color blowup of a black-necked stilt (the only one I saw that day). The type was illegibly sun-bleached—a fading screed of ornithological anachronism.

There would have been more birds if marshes and riparian woodlands, instead of hay fields and buildings, had stretched the horizons. When they did, the Bay must have been more than a way station for many shorebirds and waterfowl. There was a lot more water to produce food for them, and thus more nesting. The restored wetlands at Point Reyes support summering coots, grebes, rails, green herons, blue herons, bitterns, and wood ducks, as well as egrets and mallards.

If Frederick C. Lincoln had conceived his flyways in the sixteenth century instead of the twentieth, they might have been less elegantly tornado shaped.

Still, birds will keep coming if we let them. They are resourceful creatures, like the curlew flocks that forage many miles inland at Round Valley Regional Preserve near Brentwood each fall. In Mount Diablo's rain shadow, the oak-dotted grassland there hardly seems the place for long-billed shorebirds, but curlews eat grasshoppers as well as marsh worms and snails. Or like a pair of mallards I saw at a tiny cattle pond for a few years.

The pond dried up in summer, so they went elsewhere then, but they were back in the winter and spring. During a wet year, they raised a brood. One day, after seeing the drake on the pond, I found the female leading a troop of ducklings in a creek on the other side of the ridge above it. The next spring was a dry one, and the pond hardly held water, but the mallards still came back. I saw them one day, huddled in a cattail patch as though wondering what to do next.

—2014

the north bay

the raven roost

I usually like wind. I like to see it toss treetops and swirl leaves down a street, or hear it buffet walls, rattle windows, and howl under doors. When it blows all the time though, not in gusts and eddies but in flat streams, it can be abrasive. Walking in a steady wind all day is like lying on cold ground. The unyielding element robs the body first of warmth, then of feeling, and when feeling goes life isn't far behind. A strong steady wind dulls smell, sound, touch, and even sight if one faces into it. The walker begins to feel more like a rock or a ghost than a living being.

The wind blows like that a lot at a big raven roost on Point Reyes. A long valley runs up from Drakes Estero, and ocean wind flows unhindered there. The wind itself might have carved the valley: the hills and rocks look as shaved and huddled as the coyote bush scrub and willow thickets. The roost occupies a pine plantation on the marshy flat just above the water. Many of the pines are dead, gray skeletons, which enhances the spectral impression.

The wind didn't bother me at first when I visited the roost one sunny March afternoon. The ravens hadn't returned for the night: I walked under the pines looking for signs of the birds but finding only one black feather. I did find a long-dead fox, a recently dead mouse, and a surprising number of mushrooms—clusters of slender reddish gill mushrooms; clumps of wrinkled black-and-white false morels, or "elfin saddles"; yellow shelves of bracket fungus. It seemed that the introduced Monterey pines had brought their symbiotic mycorrhizal fungi with them. Or maybe they hadn't, since so many trees were dying. Maybe the mushrooms were mostly parasites.

When I walked out the other side of the plantation, I found a deer browsing the turf. It didn't see me, but a pair of ravens on a distant hillside did. The big black birds took wing, and one flew toward me and hovered overhead, croaking. The deer fled, and the ravens veered away out of sight.

I'd started to feel the wind by then, and although the pines offered some shelter, it was good to get back into sunlight.

I went down to the water to eat lunch, but the wind picked up sandwiches, celery sticks, oatmeal cookies, and thermos cup and flung them to the sand ten feet away. After scrambling to catch them and gingerly eating the gritty fragments, I was sleepy, but the wind wouldn't even let me take a nap in peace. It plucked at my clothes like an importunate brat, startling me awake and snatching away the sun's warmth.

AEROBATICS

I'd come to the roost looking for insight into a mentality that is a strange mix of openness and elusiveness. I'd been interested in ravens since reading T. H. White's account of their flying prowess in *The Once and Future King*: he calls them the best of all fliers. Growing up in New England, I couldn't watch them, but California offered many chances to do so. When I lived in Sonoma County, a flock roosted in some Douglas firs nearby, and I'd sit in the grove and listen to them croaking to one another. It was like listening to people calling back and forth from different rooms of a house. The calls had the absentminded tone of people talking while absorbed in other matters.

Later, walking in Golden Gate National Recreation Area's Tennessee Valley, I came within ten feet of a pair sitting on a fence. It was foggy, but the ravens didn't seem to mind my appearance out of the mist. A calf also watched them—from a few inches away—but they ignored it too. They were neatly butchering and eating two rodents, probably pocket gophers. Each removed the head, swallowed that, opened the abdomen with a sharp hook at the end of its beak, discarded the viscera, and swallowed the rest. After both birds finished, the smaller one made soft "craw-craw-craw" sounds that prompted the larger to fly to the same post. They huddled together a moment, and the smaller one put its beak under the larger one's and then reached up and touched the top of its head. Both birds blinked, bluish eye membranes sliding over shiny black pupils in a way that seemed curiously vulnerable. Then they shied at my presence and flew away.

Walking on a ridgetop above Tennessee Valley some days later, I saw a raven pair land on a fence on another ridge. Two more arrived, and they all flew to the ground and began turning over cow flops, probably looking for insects. They flew away when I walked toward them but then reappeared above the knoll I stood on and began an aerial dance, as though to show off. They circled in the air current that rose above the knoll, barely flapping their wings, just adjusting their tails, rudder-fashion, as they swept silently back and forth, up and down, twenty feet above my head. They would rise, side slip, cross each other's wakes, then swoop and rise again. They let their claws hang loose, like human acrobats resting hands on hips while doing handsprings on a high wire.

The performance clearly excited them, and it sped up. One bird croaked several times, as if exhilarated, and they paired off. Each pair flew close, one above the other, and they made little swoops, emitting high-pitched liquid sounds, like rain in a gutter. That ended the performance, and they all soared away on the updraft, still barely moving their wings. A moment later, they returned to the knoll, and one dropped to the ground and grabbed something. The other three landed with it as it went through the butchering and eating process I'd watched before, although they were impatient and finally left, hastily followed by the other.

I wanted to see more raven behavior, so I thought I should start at the beginning and watch them at a nest. When I asked at the Point Reyes Bird Observatory, however, they told me that they didn't know where ravens nested and that there were no recent records of ravens nesting at Point Reyes or even in Marin County. This seemed incredible for such a common bird. The ornithologists thought perhaps they nested in sea cliffs or big trees but had no recent evidence of it. They did tell me how to find the roost in the pine plantation, known since at least 1941: that's how I arrived there on the windy March afternoon.

THE FLYING CIRCUS

After my attempted nap, I spent the rest of the afternoon wandering the hills, vainly seeking windless spots, mentally shivering as emerald green chorus frogs hopped into cow-trampled mires. The sun got lower and weaker. I was surprised when I came to a ridgetop in sight of the roost and saw a dense cloud of ravens billowing around an isolated Monterey cypress near the pines. There may have been a hundred, and I could see more circling a cliff on the other side of the valley. I had no idea where they'd all come from (although the ones I'd seen in Tennessee Valley had disappeared at that time of day).

From my experience at Tennessee Valley, I thought I'd see even more raven behavior in this huge crowd, but I'd misunderstood their protocols. The birds in the pines at the roost kept their distance, although perhaps more from lack of interest than fear of an intruder. I was glad they didn't seem to mind me, given the dozens of hooked, hatchet-sized beaks circling around me or perched in the pines. But they were involved in their own interactions, isolating me deftly if I approached them, like people excluding a bore at a party. If I trained my binoculars on one, it would move, apparently sensing it was in the frame somehow.

It was too cold to stand watching, so I crossed the dam to the cliff, where many ravens still circled. Colors intensified as the sun neared the horizon—red cliff, blue water, black birds. Even the mudflats glowed a bright chocolate purple. The ravens circled so high that they appeared no larger than swallows, but their swarming was more deliberate and complex than swallows'. A pair flew in tandem; then one bird suddenly flipped on its back, so the two flew breast to breast. They did a roll, a dive, and a swoop too fast for my eye to follow, then flew into another group and changed partners. Nearby, two birds tried flying with the same partner. One of the apparent rivals dived at the other, which did an aerial somersault and flew off in the opposite direction. One bird carried a stone in one claw, dropped it, swooped and caught it in its beak, then dropped and caught it again. The wealth of virtuoso performances was bewildering.

Ravens seem the most consciously aerobatic of birds, unsurpassed for general aerial dexterity. I've seen them flying circles around hawks and eagles. While the raptors soared in their effortless arcs, the ravens effortlessly flew arcs within arcs, occasionally rising above the hawks to swoop at them. The hawks kept circling higher, trying to escape, but the ravens followed until they disappeared. (Blackbirds and kingbirds mob ravens, however: the big birds flinch and squawk ignobly as the small ones torment them.)

We don't know how ravens arrived at this command of the sky. Humans may know less about them now than we did ten thousand years ago. They loomed large in the folklore of the prehistoric people who inhabited their circumpolar range. One Native American tribe professed to understand many of their varied, polysyllabic cries. Although science has produced raven statistics, I doubt if our systematic knowledge goes much deeper than our ancestors' experiential lore. We know how many eggs ravens are likely to lay (four or seven) but less about where and how they lay them. According to one ornithological faction, ravens are among the most highly evolved birds because they have the largest cerebral hemispheres in relation to size of all birds. According to another, they are among the most primitive birds because of their relatively unspecialized plumage.

The ravens were still at it when I left at dusk. The wind was even colder in the dark, and getting into the car was like climbing into a boat after swimming too long in cold water. I think the ravens enjoy the wind though. Few creatures are better adapted to that anarchic element, which gives the big black birds an alien quality that is surprising when many live so close to millions of humans.

—*Berkeley Monthly*, July 1981

the mount vision fire

The Phillip Burton Wilderness in Point Reyes National Seashore is one of the most heavily visited areas in the U.S. wilderness system, for good reasons. It's the only unit that is an hour's drive from the Bay Area and one of very few that border the ocean. Its mosaic of habitats—from beaches, to coastal scrub and prairie, to riparian thickets, to old-growth Douglas fir and hardwood forest, to ridgetop grasslands—provides a diversity of wildlife and scenery that would be extraordinary anywhere. So close to a megalopolis, it's miraculous.

In the three decades I've been visiting the Burton, I've seen it change considerably. Many changes have been positive. Native shrubs and grasses have reclaimed weedy pastures. Riparian vegetation has covered eroded streambeds. Wildlife populations have grown. The bobcat population in the wilderness is phenomenal. I see one or more bobcats about every other visit. Other changes in recent years have made me wonder about the future. Trails are deteriorating under heavy use. Mountain bike tracks are everywhere, despite NO BIKE signs on foot and horse trailheads. Horseback use—particularly around the Five Brooks area— is such that stretches of trail are deep in dust in the summer and fall and in mud in the winter and spring. I sympathize with the Park Service in dealing with these impacts. Horseback riding is a legitimate use, and mountain bikers are hard to control. Anyway, they probably don't threaten the wilderness area's overall ecological quality.

Ironically, a natural process now under way in the Burton could affect some aspects of ecological quality significantly. Douglas fir is invading forest glades, coastal prairies, and other habitats, including bishop pine groves in the area's north end. This invasion is fascinating to watch, as thousands of little firs suddenly cover the bare slopes of Mount Wittenberg, the glades along the Woodward Valley Trail, and the grassy slopes at the ocean end of the Bear Valley Trail. The implication for someone who likes the present mosaic of forest and open habitat can be unsettling though. In another decade or two, much of the present grassland and scrub in the Burton may look like a tree farm.

To be sure, much of the Burton *is* former tree farm. A lot of Douglas fir was planted during various commercial reforestation projects or grew naturally after logging in the 1950s. And the Burton's scrub and grasslands also reflect past human activity— the decades of ranching before the seashore's establishment in 1962 and the many centuries during which the native Miwoks managed the land to foster game and food plants.

There's not too much protected Douglas fir forest in the world today, so there would be positive aspects to letting reversion go on at Point Reyes. Yet I think some things might be lost in the process, and not only from the human viewpoint. I don't think bobcats would benefit particularly from a tree farm state of forest reversion. Most bobcats I've seen in the Burton have been in grass or scrub, where the gophers, rabbits, quail, and voles are. There would be bobcats in a tree farm Burton, but perhaps not as many. There might be fewer badgers, burrowing owls, and other interesting creatures. There would be fewer poppies, lupines, tidy tips, brodiaeas, goldenrods, asters, and other grassland wildflowers.

Of course, reversing Douglas fir invasion of open habitats would require either human intervention or wildfire, neither of which seems altogether desirable in a wilderness area so near a megalopolis. At present, the Park Service is letting reversion proceed more or less freely. In the past few years, they've done small controlled burns at Divide Meadow on Bear Valley Trail, mainly to eradicate a patch of Scotch broom (an exotic weed that Douglas fir reversion would eradicate anyway). They put out a wild brush fire south of Coast Camp with fire lines and chemical retardant.

Worrying about Douglas fir reversion may seem trivial when human activities threaten wilderness everywhere. Yet California's high biodiversity is a result of the kind of habitat mosaics that are starting to dwindle in the Burton. The situation there isn't unique to California, where sub-urban growth around wilderness areas makes fire unpopular both in its wild state and as a management tool. Still, I bet most hikers would prefer a mixture of forest, glades, meadows, and brushy slopes to one of Douglas fir forest and saplings. Since the Burton is one of very few ocean-bordering wilderness areas, people like to see the water.

AFTER

Little did I know—when I wrote a piece last year about encroachment of Douglas fir forest on other habitats at the Phil Burton Wilderness on Point Reyes—how soon nature and some high school campers would address the matter—or how near apocalyptically. An early October wildfire that started at an abandoned campfire on Mount Vision west of Inverness burned most of the wilderness area's north half, consuming eleven thousand acres and destroying forty-eight homes at a cost of well over $20 million in damage alone.

I walked around the southern part of the burned area after the Park Service reopened it in mid-November. As I stood on the Coast Trail midway between Arch Rock and Coast Camp, all the land in sight was burned. It was a magnificent spectacle—in an austere way even a lively one. A lot of raptors and songbirds were flying about, and insects, particularly butterflies, were even more abundant. The only living nonavian vertebrate, however, was a young alligator lizard on the trunk of a huge old eucalyptus (unharmed by the fire except for dead lower limbs and charred bark) at a homestead site above Kelham Beach. Many bones lay around, exposed when the grass burned off. Most looked old, although I saw one fresh deer skeleton, either a fire casualty or a lion kill.

The contrast between the fire's behavior in coastal scrub-grassland and fir forest was striking. It had burned grass and scrub so uniformly that the effect was rather tidy; fir forest so nonuniformly that the effect was chaotic—almost whimsical.

At first, the grass, scrub, and riparian woods of the headlands and coastal slopes resembled the pre-fire scattering of light and dark vegetation—until I saw that the light patches were bare soil instead of grass, while the dark ones were charred sticks instead of brush. Along creeks, the fire had baked the leaves of bay, buckthorn, and wax myrtle to a light orange color. The landscape was like a photo negative of its pre-fire self. Having burned uniformly, the scrub and grassland were starting to regenerate that way. All the coyote bushes had an inch of new growth at the base, and bracken ferns a foot tall grew from the blackened soil. Perennial native grasses like purple needlegrass and California fescue were sprouting from their root bases.

The only scrub-grassland that hadn't burned was the headland south of Coast Camp that had burned the year before. Although the coyote bush there had regrown to a couple of feet high and timothy and other grasses grew densely, the Mount Vision Fire merely scorched the ground and a scattering of bushes. It left the dry grass unburned. Evidently there wasn't enough fuel for it.

The fire's effect on the Douglas fir forest of Inverness Ridge was obvious from the reddish brown of dead treetops all along the ridge and in the ravines below. But the dead foliage mixed with living green foliage in a disorderly way, quite unlike the tidy scrub-grassland. When I climbed Inverness Ridge and walked through the forest on the Woodward Valley Trail, it confirmed the impression. Sometimes the fire had burned only the ground, sometimes only the tree trunks, sometimes only the foliage. I passed one place where it had charred an open grove of good-sized firs but had left untouched an adjacent thicket of saplings that seemed much more vulnerable.

The fire did have the predictable effect of erasing most of the young firs that had become established on the upper slopes of the scrub-grassland and of opening up the largely even-aged forest on the ridgetop, much of which was planted during reforestation projects in the 1930s. It didn't reach the grasslands around Mount Wittenberg or the meadows on the landward side of Inverness Ridge, so they continue to revert to Douglas fir.

The fire affected the wilderness area with more than its flames. The top of Inverness Ridge now looks like a post-logging tree farm instead of a pre-logging one because firefighters brought in heavy equipment to cut a break south to near Coast Camp. This was a violation of the spirit if not the letter of the Wilderness Act, but I doubt anybody thought of that in the panicky atmosphere. They were afraid the fire would crown in the old growth above Bear Valley and keep going toward Bolinas and points south. As though in mitigation of this, the Park Service has done some rehabilitation of eroded trails.

Along with hand-wringing about property damage, the media carried feel-good rhetoric about how nature is adapted to fire and will regenerate. I wonder, though, about some of the effects of such a big, rare fire on a natural area surrounded by farms and suburbs that is still recovering from two centuries of heavy livestock grazing. Exotic weeds like pampas grass and broom, and introduced forage grasses like timothy and wild oats, have regenerated as quickly as the native vegetation. They are as fire-adapted as the natives, since most come from similar Mediterranean climates.

The fire might have been less costly and destructive if the Park Service had the funds to manage vegetation more with controlled burns. At least, it might have managed the area along the Inverness residential zone, since the bishop pine habitat is fire-dependent. If it had, the fire might have stopped at the houses, which could have been worth the money, not only in short-run terms of property and public money saved but in long-run ones of learning to live with fire. Civilization will have the luxury of fighting fires with aircraft, bulldozers, and chainsaws only as long as fossil fuel is cheap and abundant enough, which, incredible as it seems, won't be forever.

—*Wilderness Record*, January 1995, December 1995

the ghost of crystal lakes

In the 1970s, it was a treat to see the fallow deer that Point Reyes National Seashore had inherited from its ranching past. The Eurasian species, introduced for hunting half a century ago, has several color phases, from white to blackish brown, and the stags have impressive antlers. A few dozen of the deer lived in the park then. Today, it's less of a treat because they're hard not to see. Their population has exploded to almost nine hundred: some meadows look like fallow deer feedlots.

Earlier this year, the Park Service announced a plan to remove fallow deer from the seashore, along with another exotic species, Asian axis deer, which number almost three hundred. They say the axis deer population could double within six years and that both species are competing with black-tailed deer and other native species, impacting adjacent ranches and threatening to spread elsewhere. I believe them.

In recent decades, I've perceived a decline in the black-tail population and even in the numbers of smaller herbivores like rabbits and jackrabbits, which also compete for browse plants with exotic deer. I've seen fewer bobcats, which live mainly on rabbits and jackrabbits. This has happened surprisingly fast. In the 1970s, large black-tail herds were common in the seashore's grasslands. As late as 1987, I recall walking north toward Bear Valley on the Earthquake Trail one June evening in what seemed a black-tail paradise, with groups of the deer scattered over the flats like antelope on African savanna. A bobcat bounded through them almost playfully. But such scenes faded after the early 1990s as fallow deer thronged the Olema Valley.

Given this situation, I think the exotic deer should be removed. But I'm glad it's not my job. Some years ago, the Park Service had to stop a culling program aimed at managing the exotics because of public displeasure orchestrated by local media. So its removal proposal is even less popular. Local homes sport big green banners proclaiming: "Manage, Don't Exterminate, Fallow Deer." I understand the sentiment. The fallow and axis deer aren't at fault, of course, and people like to have diverse faunas in wild lands. But perhaps there's a lesson in this unhappy affair: that we need to think more about biodiversity in parks.

When Congress established Point Reyes National Seashore in 1962, biologists could have foreseen that three species of medium-sized deer in the same habitat would cause problems. They could have removed the exotic species' small populations easily then. Unfortunately, we don't allow the Park Service to think ahead much because we underfund it and thus keep it busy dealing with crises that arise from lack of foresight, like the present exotic deer explosion.

When we do let the Park Service think ahead, on the other hand, the results can be positive, as with California's other native deer species, tule elk. Once abundant at Point Reyes, the elk disappeared there in the 1800s, as in most of California. Soon after the seashore's establishment, the Park Service established a fenced preserve for the species on Tomales Point. Since the elk thrived there, they were able to release a few in the seashore's Phillip Burton Wilderness Area in 1998, restoring some lost native biodiversity. The elk are a good replacement for the exotic deer.

Still, the removal of two thriving and attractive, albeit nonnative, species from the seashore raises a knotty planning question. Are black-tailed deer and tule elk really the only native wild ungulates we can have at Point Reyes and, by extension, in much of California? This question relates to a debate about the definition of "native" that has gone on for decades.

In the 1960s a national panel of scientists, the Leopold Committee, advised the Park Service to set a goal of maintaining or restoring the species that had lived in parks at the time Europeans reached the Americas. But other scientists, such as Paul S. Martin, a paleontologist at the University of Arizona, think this goal is too limited. They argue that if we are really interested in restoring natural biodiversity we should go further back in time, since the fossil record shows that North America had many more large wildlife species during the past 65 million years, the "Age of Mammals." Only in the past fifteen thousand years or so has species diversity dropped to present low levels.

The debate involving another native ungulate is already on the ground at Point Reyes. Records show that pronghorn "antelope" inhabited the Bay Area in historical times, although it is unclear if they inhabited Point Reyes then. Still, pronghorns almost certainly lived at Point Reyes sometime in the past, since they've inhabited western North America for millions of years. Should they be restored? I don't know if pronghorns could thrive at Point Reyes today. I do think Martin has a point when he says that confining park biodiversity to historic levels may be unnecessarily austere. Judging from prehistory, Point Reyes might even accommodate yet another large native ungulate besides elk and pronghorns.

There are areas of the seashore where elk don't venture and even black-tails are scarce—the old-growth Douglas fir forest in the southern half of the seashore's Phil Burton Wilderness Area. Indeed, large herbivores are scarce in most West Coast ancient forest now. Has this always been so? Not according to the fossil record, which shows that California forests contained not only extinct giants like mastodons and ground sloths but surviving species like tapirs, relatives of horses and rhinos that can weigh over five hundred pounds.

Tapirs live in South and Central American forests today, but fossils show they inhabited North American ones from 50 million years ago until the great die-off of the past fifteen thousand years. They are about as native to North America as an extirpated species can be. And, according to Martin, they disappeared not because of an environmental cause like climate change but because humans extirpated them. In that case, tapirs could live here again. The local Sierra Club chairman told the *San Francisco Chronicle* that we should remove exotic deer from Point Reyes because we imported them. Maybe we should return tapirs there because, albeit long ago, we extirpated them.

I don't know if tapirs could thrive at Point Reyes now, but there are parts of the Phil Burton Wilderness that seem to me like tapir heaven, particularly Crystal Lakes, a primeval-looking complex of marsh, ponds, and conifers in the south part of the wilderness. If there's a "place that time forgot" in the Bay Area, it is Crystal Lakes. It's a half day's hike from the Bear Valley Trailhead, and since the Park Service budget for trail maintenance is spotty, the hike can be adventurous, with some crawling through brush and climbing around fallen trees. Eventually, the trail drops into a basin that has a unique sense of secrecy and self-containment. I've been visiting it almost every year for more than a decade, but I've seldom seen anyone else there. The basin has no surface outlet, so the landscape changes continually according to the weather, which enhances the impression of discovery.

In wet periods, the spring-fed lakes grow to cover the trail, and hiking becomes wading. Then their clear depths reveal large fish that I haven't seen elsewhere—perhaps one of several primitive giant minnow species native to the Bay Area, like hitch, California roach, or thicktail chub (although the latter is considered extinct). Since the lakes are so isolated, the fish may have been there for a long time.

In dry periods, the lakes shrink to algae-dotted ponds, and Douglas firs start to grow on former lake bottom among the skeletons of the firs that grew there in previous dry periods. The fish disappear from the smaller ponds: I suppose they shelter in the deepest parts of the remaining ones. It is strange to see a landscape change so much within a few years, like a time-lapse film.

The place is a kind of diorama of forest evolution, a living version of 40-million-year-old fossil lake beds found in Wyoming, which then had a warm temperate climate and vegetation like California's now. The diorama could use some animal life besides fish, however, and although I've seen herons, ducks, coots, and other waterbirds there, I've never seen a mammal larger than a squirrel. Tapir fossils are common around those prehistoric lake deposits. Living ones certainly would be an interesting addition at Crystal Lakes.

I don't think tapirs would conflict with other park ungulates or adjacent ranches. They are shy, solitary, and slow breeding. Even where protected, they seem ghostly for such large animals, although their horselike smell can betray their presence. Most surviving tapirs inhabit tropical forest, but they also live in much cooler mountain cloud forest, so climate would not necessarily be a barrier to their living here.

Hunting and deforestation are threatening tapirs all over Latin America. The mountain tapir, a cool-weather species of the Andes, is endangered. So restoring tapirs to North America would be good long-range planning if we really do want to save large mammal biodiversity.

There could be other benefits. Having more large ungulates in the forest could enhance plant diversity and reduce potential wildfire intensity. And, along with elk and black-tailed deer in Point Reyes's more open areas, visitors might get a rare chance to glimpse an evolutionary "ghost" among its Douglas firs, maples, and oaks.

—*Los Angeles Times*, July 7, 2005

yellowstone west

bishop pine and the mount vision fire

I spent part of my childhood in farm countryside, and when I started visiting Point Reyes National Seashore in the early 1970s, the landscape from Limantour Beach up to the crest of Inverness Ridge made me nostalgic for that time, the late 1940s. The homestead sites, dammed lakes, fence lines, and old pastures of the pre-seashore days had a long-ago, storybook feeling—spider silk and thistledown drifting under banks of cumulus clouds; alder leaves shaking over creeks; flowering sweet pea vines; old man's beard lichens waving in the wind. The feeling combined with the wild ecosystem's return—deer, bobcats, hawks, quail—to make it a special place.

Yet I wasn't too clear about just what that wild ecosystem was. I knew that north-central Point Reyes supports a forest of bishop pine, *Pinus muricata*, a species confined to areas of dry, nutrient-poor soils along the Pacific Coast. Bishop pine resembles its widely planted relative, Monterey pine, but differs in bearing two needles to a fascicle instead of three and in having a much larger natural distribution. Named for San Luis Obispo (*obispo* is Spanish for "bishop"), where botanists first identified the species, it now occurs in scattered stands from Santa Barbara to Humboldt County, with an isolated population in Baja California. Fossils show that its ancestors were even more widespread during drier times over the past two to five million years.

Like Monterey pine, bishop pine is a termed a closed-cone species because its cones remain on the branches instead of opening every year to release their seeds and then falling off, as with most pine species. Closed-cone species are fire-adapted: the cones finally open when heat melts the resin that keeps them closed. Then they release their seeds. They thus depend on periodic fires for reproduction.

Granitic bedrock and proximity to the ocean (where the trees benefit from fog drip) make the Limantour area a good place for bishop pine. Hiking there in the 1970s and '80s, I saw plenty of them. Yet the stands on the crest and west slopes of Inverness Ridge seemed a little peripheral and vestigial to be considered a "bishop pine ecosystem." Point Reyes's main bishop pine forest grew on the ridge's east slopes down to Tomales Bay. I knew places along the Inverness Ridge Trail where bishop pines were large for a species that seldom grows over fifty feet tall or lives more than a century. But few young pines occurred in the underbrush of huckleberry and other shrubs, and the largest pines seemed senescent. Although hot weather or gray squirrels can open some cones, that doesn't release enough seeds to regenerate a bishop pine forest, and the pine seedlings compete poorly with other trees in their parents' shade. Saplings of hardwoods like bay laurel, wax myrtle, madrone, and live oak mainly grew under the big pines.

There were places on the ridge's west slopes where small pines predominated, but those were shallow-soiled granitic outcrops and the little pines were dwarfs, older than they looked, growing where few other woody plants could thrive. On deeper-soiled sites, Douglas fir saplings poked up everywhere among the grass and brush. Although the landscape changed little from year to year, the overall plant succession seemed to be headed toward the mixed hardwood and Douglas fir forest that grows on the sandstone and shale bedrock in the seashore south of Limantour.

Then came the wildfire of October 1995, which consumed the vegetation from Mount Vision west to Limantour Beach with astounding thoroughness. Standing on Inverness Ridge a few weeks after the fire and seeing almost nothing but blackened earth in every direction, I felt less inclined than before to take plants for granted. And the speed with which they reclaimed the area over the next few years made me take them even *less* for granted. They began to seem less vegetative and more animated—almost animal. Bracken fern and coyote bush sprouted from charred bases days after the fire. Grasses and forbs like trefoil, lupine, clover, and rush-rose covered the soil by the summer. Shrubs and vines—blue blossom ceanothus, huckleberry, salal, manroot, blackberry—shaded out many of the herbs by the summer after that. Patches of blue blossom grew six feet tall in that time. Two rare endemic shrubs, Mount Vision ceanothus and Marin manzanita, produced many seedlings for the first time in years.

No plant species in the post-fire Limantour area proved more dynamic, however, than *Pinus muricata*. The fire killed almost all the existing pines in the burn area; indeed, the pines contributed greatly to the fire's speed and intensity. A firefighter told the *San Francisco Chronicle* that they burned "like Roman candles." Yet the heat freed countless pine seeds, which can stay viable for decades within their sealed cones. Fiery updrafts sent the winged seeds showering onto the westward slopes and headlands, including many places where pines had not grown. Bishop pine seedlings started appearing a few months after the fire and a year later formed large, irregular patches in sites where grass, brush, or Douglas fir had seemed the permanent vegetation.

Those seedlings looked different from the bishop pines I'd known before. The pre-fire trees had a lot of character, both the picturesque, umbrella-shaped large specimens and the gnarled, persistent little ones. But they were a bit drab—their needles plain green; their trunks, branches, and cones grayish. The post-fire bishop pines had an electric quality, as though some plugged-in current was emanating from them, making bark and needles glow. After three years, their silvery terminal shoots, many six feet tall, began producing blue-and-purple male cones, gaudy enough for a Christmas tree.

A phenomenon in the soil may have contributed to this impression of enhanced vitality. Mycologists found that the fire stimulated a population explosion of fungi that live symbiotically on the roots of young bishop pines, helping them absorb mineral nutrients in return for photosynthesis-produced food. Uncommon before the fire (when other fungal species performed the symbiotic function for the mature trees), the young fungi—*Rhizopogon* and *Tuber*—grew abundantly from spores that had been resting in the soil for decades.

Looking east from Limantour Beach toward Inverness Ridge in 1997, I saw few of the farmland vestiges that had made me nostalgic before the fire. The burned landscape reminded me more of Yellowstone National Park after the 1987 fires there. The headlands and slopes now had a similar shaggy look, like a landscape for elk rather than cattle, and in 1998 the Park Service introduced some tule elk from the Tomales Point Preserve.

Although the flames temporarily impacted sensitive species like the aplodontia, or "mountain beaver" (not a beaver but a uniquely primitive rodent species with an isolated race endemic to Point Reyes), the post-fire landscape seemed to attract and stimulate wildlife. Butterflies and other insects thronged the burned area even before the wildflowers bloomed, as though anticipating the feast to come. One insect species, a small black moth, proved new to science.

Meadow voles underwent one of their periodic population explosions, probably encouraged by the wealth of leguminous forbs. The conical stick dens of dusky-footed wood rats appeared in the new thickets of pine and blue blossom with surprising speed, considering how vulnerable that species is to fire. Dens become virtual funeral pyres for their sedentary occupants during wildfires, but the species recolonized the area abundantly, taking advantage of new shrub growth. Predators in turn took advantage of open ground and rodent abundance. Coyotes became more common. Soon after the fire, I had my first and only sighting of a golden eagle—rare at Point Reyes—in the seashore. I also saw a long-tailed weasel near Limantour, the only one I've seen in that part of the park.

There was no doubt after the Vision Fire that the Limantour area is a bishop pine ecosystem, just as there was no doubt after its 1987 fires that most of Yellowstone is a lodgepole pine ecosystem, also dependent on fire for renewal. Visiting Yellowstone after that fire, I saw aspen sprouting everywhere, as I saw blue blossom ceanothus sprouting everywhere at post-fire Point Reyes. Both species had dwindled to senescent remnants before the fire, and the renewal of both benefited important rodents—beavers at Yellowstone, wood rats at Point Reyes. They in turn benefited wildlife generally. Beaver ponds provide habitat for otters, muskrats, herons, ducks, turtles, and many other creatures. Wood rat dens shelter mice, lizards, and salamanders.

I understand better how *Pinus muricata*'s ancestor thrived in a prehistoric landscape that included mammoths, saber-toothed cats, and ground sloths, as well as the surviving elk, deer, and mountain lions. Such giants wouldn't look out of place there now. As the last ranching-era vestiges have vanished, roads revegetated, dammed lakes and hay fields reverted to marshes and riparian woodland, I've sometimes missed my pre-fire nostalgia, but not that much. Bishop pine forest seems right for the place, although the wildfire on which it depends for renewal can be catastrophic. Still, whether started by an illegal campfire like the Vision Fire or by more natural factors, wildfires are inevitable, like earthquakes. We just have to adapt to life's dangers in the end, like all the other organisms.

The thousands of teenaged bishop pines now growing from Limantour Beach to the Inverness Ridge Trail are vivid reminders of that fact, although the landscape doesn't look quite as shaggy now as it did in 1997. In fact, some of it resembles a 1950s Weyerhaeuser tree farm ad, as the even-aged pines give the slopes an almost industrially regular look. Some hikers find the close-growing young forest claustrophobic and monotonous compared to the panoramas that the Bucklin and Drakes View Trails offered before the fire. But time is opening the forest as weaker trees die, and diversity is increasing as ferns, vines, shrubs, and hardwoods invade the understory, exploiting coppery patches of sunlight that penetrate the canopy. Native bunchgrasses and wildflowers thrive in glades and open headlands: even in midsummer—when most of the Bay Area is baked brown—deep blue gentians, "Martian eyeball" heleniums, and ladies' tresses orchids bloom among the more common scarlet paintbrushes and yellow hawksweeds.

Above, where their needles endlessly sing in the wind, the little pines' two-foot-long, silver-and-amber terminal shoots still seem to glow from within. Female cones in various stages of development—bright green new ones, year-old orange ones, weathered gray ones—ring the trunks and branches, patiently awaiting the next wildfire.

—*Bay Nature*, July–September 2012

the east bay

grasslands

One of the few places I know in the Bay Area that resembles California's original native grasslands is a hillside behind the East Bay Regional Park office on Skyline Boulevard in Oakland. From a distance, the east-facing hill looks like any other grassy slope around here—green in winter, brown in summer—but a closer look reveals something different from the wild oats, foxtail, mustard, and thistles that cover most California hillsides now. Native bunchgrasses and wildflowers cover this slope, and every time I go there, it seems, I find new species of them.

Last June, the slope was studded with yellow mariposa tulips, lily-family flowers aptly described by their name's double reference to tulips and butterflies. Usually found in relatively undisturbed grasslands, they are an uncommon sight in the Bay Area today. Even thicker on the hillside were lacy, white-flowered tarweeds, sunflower-family plants named for sticky secretions that protect their leaves and stems from hot season desiccation, allowing them to flower throughout it. And almost as abundant as these flowers were chalcedony checkerspots, red, black, and white butterflies clustering so thickly on some plants that I at first thought they were big showy blossoms themselves.

Many wildflower species that had peaked earlier in the spring were still in bloom: fiery California poppy, blue lupine and Ithuriel's spear, bright pink farewell-to-spring. I found many seedpods of blue-eyed grass, a small iris relative that had covered the hillside in April and May, when low-growing patches of goldfields, another sunflower relative, had bloomed even more thickly. "Goldfields" is an apt name: the little bright yellow flowers literally form fields of gold if conditions are right.

Native grass species covered the hillside even more thickly than wildflowers, from big, droopy California fescue with flowering stems up to my chest, to medium-sized wild rye, to smaller purple needlegrass. I could name only these most common ones. Most had already passed the flowering stage, and the only way to definitely identify many grass species is to dissect the florets and key them out according to details in structure. Regional park botanists have identified some fifteen native grass species on the few acres of hillside, including pine bluegrass, brome, melic, and bentgrass, as well as the ones I recognized.

Botanists think native plants survive there for a paradoxical reason—because the soil is bad. The bedrock is serpentine, a rock with a chemical composition that makes it not only infertile but even toxic to the aggressive Old World weeds that have taken over better soils in most of California. Many natives are adapted to serpentine, however, so the exotics are unable to move in and crowd them out. The apparently tranquil hillside is a kind of botanical Indian reservation, natives holding onto a piece of ground that invaders aren't able to exploit.

California's Native Americans and the grasslands from which they drew much of their food and fiber were thriving when European colonists arrived. Colonization reduced both to scattered survivors within little more than a century, one of history's human and botanical tragedies and one that raises a troubling ecological and evolutionary question. If the natives were well adapted to their environment, how could invaders replace them so quickly? How could organisms that had evolved halfway across the planet overcome organisms evolved here during thousands of years? This situation seems to transgress the idea—important to the conservation movement—that survival depends on adaptation to the environment.

History shows how Native Americans succumbed to invasion. First, Old World diseases to which they had no resistance decimated them, and then colonists destroyed their culture and environment. Wheat fields and livestock replaced their native grasslands and game, and when they tried to defend their livelihood, colonists murdered many and drove survivors onto missions and reservations.

History is less clear about the causes of native grasslands' destruction. Old World plant diseases and pests may have affected them, but I haven't seen documentation of this, although alien diseases are known to threaten many native tree and shrub species. Colonists certainly decimated native grasses and wildflowers by turning most of California into farms and towns. Yet wild oats, foxtail fescue, mustard, and thistles also invaded parts of the state where native grasslands were never plowed or paved. And although livestock overgrazing and drought certainly contributed to the destruction, botanists don't think they were completely responsible for it. They think the exotic annuals were more efficient at growing and reproducing here than the native perennials.

In fact, weed-grown land that is withdrawn from grazing often just keeps producing exotic annuals for the most part. In some once-grazed natural areas like Mount Diablo State Park, many natives still bloom abundantly among the wild oats, foxtail, and filaree. In others, like Briones Regional Park, native grasses and wildflowers have virtually disappeared, although native trees and shrubs still thrive. Botanists have failed to find more than a few acres that might be called "virgin" California grassland. Jepson Prairie in Solano County is one of these rare sites, but when I visited it one spring day, it was hard to distinguish from surrounding pastures. Except for some goldfields and blue *Downingia* around vernal pools, I saw few flowers among the grasses. It was less showy than the little hillside behind the Regional Parks office.

The situation is puzzling. Gardeners who plant native "wildflower mix" in the hope of restoring local plants to their property may get colorful masses of poppies, lupines, baby blue eyes, and other species the first year but find that weeds have reclaimed the plot the next. Perhaps such soils have lost the symbiotic fungi that would allow the natives to reclaim them. But that's not clear.

It's hard to say what might happen if weedy land were left undisturbed for centuries. Native perennials might eventually outlast exotic annuals. For the present, it seems to be a matter of "survival of the fittest," with more annual weeds surviving than native perennials. Yet evolutionary thinking has gone beyond equating "fitter" with "better," and it would be wrong to dismiss California native grasslands. For one thing, we don't know what values they may have. Civilization has swept them aside so abruptly that they've hardly had a chance to show their potential. A native grass recently discovered in the Mexican mountains is a perennial relative of annual maize, offering the possibility of cornfields that wouldn't have to be plowed up every year. Even without such sensational attributes, beauty and ecological significance are worth perpetuating. Once I learned how interesting and diverse the natives are, the sight of hillside after hillside covered with wild oats, foxtail, and filaree got very depressing.

Native grasslands can be restored. Midwesterners have restored much tallgrass prairie, an ecosystem as decimated by farming and alien weeds as California bunchgrass lands. Today, midwestern park agencies generally have prairie restoration programs. One that I worked for in Ohio—not exactly a "big sky" state—has one. They first plow and burn the weeds off a likely field, then seed it with native tall grasses like big bluestem, Indian grass, and switchgrass, and perennial wildflowers like blazing star, rattlesnake master, royal catchfly, purple coneflower, and compass plant. These are magnificent plants, some of which grow ten feet tall. Once a prairie forms, they burn it again every few years to keep weeds and trees from reinvading, since enough rainfall occurs that forest would predominate without the fires. They burn in spring, when danger of fire spreading is lowest. Ohio's original prairies burned almost every spring from lightning fires.

Restoring native grassland in semiarid California is more complicated. Native Americans managed grasslands with fire as well as selective gathering of food and fiber plants, and there have been attempts to use fire management in places where exotics still predominated after grazing stopped, but results are patchy. A close look at fire-managed places reveals natives mixed in with the weeds, especially in rocky or thin-soiled places where there is less competition. The overall impression is still mostly of wild oats, mustards, and thistles, however. In wet years, the weeds get tall; in dry years, they get small, but any changes toward native recovery must be proceeding very slowly. And even controlled burns are risky in California with its air pollution and urban wildfire disasters. So there hasn't been a consistent effort to use that tool, in the Bay Area at least.

Carefully controlled livestock grazing can benefit native grassland by thinning exotic grasses and allowing more space for natives. But it's hard to limit economically hard-pressed ranching operations, and grazing doesn't help grasslands where natives are already gone. Maybe more intensive efforts on a smaller scale might work—perhaps just having volunteers clear some weedy plots to plant and tend natives. It would be good if every Bay Area park had some mariposa tulips in June, when the wild oats are dead and brown.

—*Berkeley Monthly*, November 1979

life in the cemetery

Mountain View Cemetery above Piedmont Avenue in Oakland probably matches any place in the Bay Area for volume of plant and animal life. It is tended well enough to keep the ornamental plants healthy but not so well as to exclude a lot of wild plants, native and feral. Many are good food sources—the place is a delicatessen of exotic fare for local wildlife. A hummingbird can choose from Australian eucalyptus, South American fuchsia, Asian pittosporum, and African acacia, as well as California monkey flower. In winter, Anna's hummingbirds sing squeakily from the eucalyptus, joined in spring by the migratory Allen's hummingbirds that take possession of the shrubbery.

Abundance brings competition. Three-inch hummingbirds don't hesitate to claim hundred-foot trees, and they have a lot of trespassers to deal with. Flocks of cedar waxwings and robins appear in winter to eat blackberry, pyracantha, cotoneaster, and ivy berries; chickadees, titmice, and nuthatches eat insects as well as fruits; goldfinches, mourning doves, and quail go for seeds. There's competition for some prize throughout the year. Doves and quail, proverbially so gentle, are particularly combative. The mammals squabble a lot too. Once a vole tumbled out of a burrow at my feet, ejected by another mouse, which stuck its head out and eyed me a moment, as if wanting to see me off too. Another time the wild oats were alive with shrews (a tiny gray species called the ornate shrew) that chased each other around like Keystone Kops.

The cemetery's invertebrates are even more frenetic. I once watched several male wolf spiders competing for a female on a fallen tombstone. Male spiders are skinny dwarfs compared to females, but they compensate for their size with energy. These males ran in circles and jumped up and down on each other in their excitement. When the stout female ventured out of her hole under the stone, one of them would rush down and wave his pedipalps (his copulatory organs) in her face, thus inhibiting her from eating him. The pair would then zip under the stone together. A few minutes later the female would emerge to choose another suitor. I didn't see any of the chosen suitors again.

Two pairs of raptors preside over all this: one of red-tailed hawks and one of kestrels, small falcons. They are glad to take advantage of an unwary vole or songbird in the throes of competition. I've seen neatly removed quail skins beside the cemetery drives and kestrels administering the coup de grâce to victims on tombstones. The kestrels resent the hawks and spend a lot of time scolding and chasing them during mating season. Of avian predators, only the scrub and Steller's jays seem to waste little time squabbling, instead keeping sharp eyes on the main chance. I've seen a Steller's jay pluck a chickadee nestling from a tree hole and swallow it in one gulp.

It is easy to overlook all this and experience the cemetery as a dignified retreat, which it is. Still, the biotic turmoil in a place of eternal repose can skew the expectations people usually bring to necropolises. One marble monument proclaims: "Earth itself is not the goal, but stepping stone for Man," but gophers have undermined the massive stone, and it has a precarious tilt. Some smaller stones have almost sunk out of sight. Depending on point of view, the avowedly rising, actually sinking monuments might symbolize either earthly transience or the difficulty of disentangling human aspirations from more mundane evolutionary origins. The quail and mourning doves that hurtle through the stately avenues of mausoleums might be liberated souls until they land and start to gobble seeds and defecate on headstones.

The cemetery can embody a kind of earthly eternity as well as a heavenly one. A large marble fountain overlooks it, one of those Victorian wedding cake affairs with ascending tiers of small basins that drip into a large basin at ground level. When I first saw it, the small basins were mini-marshes of cattails and sedges grown from windborne seeds, and the large basin was full of green algae and tiny killifish, presumably arrived there as eggs on the feet of birds that came to bathe or drink.

One day I found it drained, and the basins cleaned of mud and plants. But when I returned again, surprisingly soon afterward, I found that, with the water turned back on, the cattails and sedges had come back. Killifish remained absent from the large basin, but something equally interesting had arrived. Aquatic snails with golden spiral shells were floating upside down at the surface, feeding on algae. They swam by, undulating the muscular "feet" on which land snails crawl.

The undulating snail feet looked like amorphous wings, and it was mesmerizing to see creatures usually associated with the most earthbound existence "flying" in a place that had been dry and lifeless shortly before. The floating, sunlit snails made life's transience seem not all that unattractive. Why ask more of the universe than a little while of floating and feeding between the ground and the sky? We humans worry about the shortness of their lives, but I think it is the length of them that really bothers us.

Whatever their viewpoint, I think most people today would agree that cemeteries, especially beautiful historic ones like Mountain View (designed in 1863 by Frederick Law Olmsted, who also created Manhattan's Central Park), are as much for the living as the dead. They are a measure of earthly wealth for one thing—idling valuable real estate for sentiment. In India, the authorities clear cemeteries left by the British Raj for more practical purposes, stacking the ornate headstones in alleys. That's too unsentimental for me. When I walk in Mountain View, I like to regard the dead as my benefactors, generous landlords of the quiet greenery and its noisy inhabitants.

—Berkeley Monthly, 1980

the peak of unexpectedness

mount diablo

I spent a night on Mount Diablo during a hot spell in August 1973. Utterly still in the afternoon's 101-degree heat, the campsite erupted at dusk with a surprisingly deafening cacophony of chirps, trills, crackles, hoots, whistles, rattles, and howls. A scent of dust and sulfur hung in the air, which stayed hot into the small hours as bats, apparently the only quiet night denizens, fluttered overhead. The dusty air obscured the stars and made the night seem infernally dark. Daylight's bucolic setting of picnic tables and barbecue grills had turned into something more like "Night on Bald Mountain" in Disney's *Fantasia*, wherein a nocturnal peak spews out swarms of demons.

Of course, demons were not making the racket: ground crickets, tree crickets, and shield-backed grasshoppers were—accompanied in the distance by owls, poorwills, and coyotes. But the inoffensive insects still seemed a bit demonic when I tracked them down in the dark. Waving their improbably long antennae, unperturbed by my flashlight, they just kept on making incredible noise, trying to attract females.

I thought of something Thoreau wrote: "Is not the midnight like Central Africa to most?" A half hour's drive from the San Ramon Valley's bustling suburbs, I was surrounded by an array of organisms as untamed and diverse as those in many more remote places.

The mountain isn't always as boisterous as it was that night, but there's usually something happening, and it's often surprising. Fence lizards are a common sight on rocks along the trails, but I didn't expect to see one dive into Pine Creek and swim off downstream like a small alligator, as I did during one wet spring. In another wet year, as I waded a pool that had flooded part of North Peak Trail, I saw what appeared to be dozens of tiny squid suspended in the water. A closer look revealed that they weren't squid but something almost as unexpected—shrimp. Although not closely related to their edible marine cousins, these little creatures are also crustaceans, called fairy shrimp because of their delicate, colorful bodies. They live in temporary spring pools only long enough to breed. Then their eggs survive in the soil, sometimes for years, until heavy rains re-create the vernal pools wherein their short life cycle unfolds.

Plants can be surprising too. Seeing a particularly gorgeous patch of red and blue wildflowers on a sunny ridge, I assumed they were California poppies and lupines, the more common spring blossoms. A closer look revealed that two much less common plants—wind poppies and Chinese houses—had made the mass of color visible from hundreds of feet away. Wind poppies may appear in abundance after fires, but that didn't explain the purplish-blue masses of Chinese houses, which usually grow scattered in shady places. Fires are generally a good source of plant surprises on the mountain, as when a wildflower called whispering bells covers blackened chaparral with masses of greenish gold in spring following a blaze.

The surprises aren't always so welcome. Walking beside the Pine Canyon cattail marsh one spring day, I realized I was passing a rattle-snake at the marsh's edge. My wife was coming a few paces behind me, so I called softly to warn her, not wanting to alarm the snake. She didn't hear me and kept coming, but we apparently hadn't surprised the rattler. It was calmly crawling back into the cattails.

There are mutual surprises with jumpier denizens. Walking the trail from Curry Point to Frog Pond one May morning, I was startled to see six half-grown coyote pups trot out of an arroyo that evidently contained a den. They were startled too—at least five of them were. They hightailed it back into the arroyo. The sixth didn't notice me and blithely trotted away along the trail. Another time, a bobcat that suddenly appeared around a bend in the Pine Canyon trail started when it saw me, but then it decided that business somehow outweighed caution in this case and kept forward on the trail. Its only concession to prudence was a short detour into the trees as it passed me. I wondered what was so important about the business. I had encountered a confused-looking, half-grown bob kitten earlier, so the business might have involved that, but it was hard to see exactly how.

Sometimes reasons for unexpected behavior are more apparent, as when I surprised a coyote pair in a chaparral gulch near the temporarily snow-covered summit one winter. They sat tight and barked at me like watchdogs instead of running away. I surmised they had a den of newborn pups there.

Even Mount Diablo's name came as a surprise. "Devil Mountain" sounds just like what Spanish missionaries might have called the East Bay's main peak, perhaps after an Indian legend. Native Americans did have many stories about the mountain, which they considered a powerful, mysterious place that had played a part in the world's creation. The local Miwok tribelet, the Volvon or Bolbones, had a village southeast of the mountain and hunted and gathered on its slopes. (The mortars they dug into rock formations to grind acorns remain in some canyons.) But, because of its religious significance, they didn't have permanent settlements on the mountain. Other groups such as the Central Valley Wintun revered the peak and visited it for religious reasons because it is so plainly visible from its environs.

In the 1700s, the Spanish explorers Pedro Fages and Juan Bautista de Anza predictably named the mountain Cerro Alto de Los Bolbones, the Bolbones' Peak. The present name originated some years later from a surprising confusion. Around 1805, some Indians fleeing captivity at a mission eluded Spanish soldiers in a willow thicket just northwest of what is now Concord. The soldiers dubbed the place El Monte de Diablo—"the devil's woodland"—perhaps because they thought the devil had helped the Indians escape or perhaps simply to express frustration. As it happens, *monte* can mean either "woodland" or "mountain." A Mexican ranch later took the name, although it wasn't associated with the mountain. Mexicans hunted and ran livestock on the peak, but it still remained too remote for settlement.

By the 1830s, however, Americans had begun to acquire land around the mountain and, confusing the former Spanish meaning with the latter, had started calling it Mount Diablo. In 1851, since it was the region's most prominent peak, the government made this official by adopting the summit as the first meridian for establishing property boundaries throughout northern California. In the 1860s, California state naturalists arrived to explore the mountain's geology and botany as well as its geography. There were surprises about those as well.

BIRTH OF A MOUNTAIN

Mount Diablo's summit is so high and isolated—with views east to the Sierra's snowy peaks and west to the Farallon Islands—that people often assume it is a volcano like Mount Lassen, also visible from the summit on clear days. When geologists explored the peak, however, they found that it is not a volcanic cone of lava and ash erupted from the earth in relatively recent times. "The material of which it is composed is extremely variable in its lithological character," wrote Josiah Whitney, head of the California State Geological Survey, in 1865, "but it consists essentially of a central portion of very hard metamorphic sandstone." Metamorphic sandstone usually forms on the seabed, which implies that Mount Diablo is a slab of ancient Pacific Ocean floor that has risen above what is now sea level. In fact, it is such a slab, although most of it is not sandstone but something more unexpected from a nineteenth-century viewpoint.

Early geologists like Whitney thought that earth's oceans and continents had always occupied their present positions. But, if so, how did ancient seabed rise to Mount Diablo's present elevation of 3,849 feet above sea level? It took the late-twentieth-century theory of plate tectonics to explain this. The theory maintains that continents and oceans have been shifting throughout the planet's existence, borne by the enormous tectonic plates that comprise earth's crust. According to the theory, the rocks that Whitney first described on Diablo's summit originated far out in the Pacific during the dinosaur age, the Jurassic and early Cretaceous periods, as lava from undersea eruptions mixed with material from earth's upper mantle to form the ocean floor. These eruptions occurred in "spreading zones," where tectonic plates originate and from which they spread out like conveyer belts as more volcanic material rises. It was the eastward spreading of one such plate—the Farallon Plate—that gradually carried the seabed rocks here.

While it spread, the Farallon Plate carried more than volcanic and mantle material. As it inched eastward during the ensuing hundred million years, the siliceous skeletons of planktonic microorganisms called radiolarians accumulated as deep sediments on the ocean floor. Heat and pressure slowly metamorphosed them into chert, a flinty, purplish rock now common on the mountain. Then, as the eastward movement continued toward another, westward-moving plate (called the North American Plate because our continent rests on it), sand and mud eroded from the land also accumulated as sediments, eventually forming other common metamorphic rocks such as schist.

All this material eventually rose above sea level through a startling tectonic process. Where the two plates collided, the North American Plate rode over the Farallon Plate, causing its subduction back into the hot, plastic mantle. The subduction process scraped much of the seabed material that had accumulated on the Farallon Plate onto North America's western edge, forming a mélange of rocks called the Franciscan Complex, which comprises much of California's coast. By 30 to 25 million years ago, the North American Plate had "consumed" the Farallon Plate through the subduction process and a northwest-moving plate, the Pacific Plate, had replaced the Farallon at the plate boundary. A lateral "strike-slip" movement then took the place of subduction as the Pacific Plate slid sideways along the North American Plate.

About three million years ago, the sliding movement between the plates changed in a way that added an element of compression, in effect squeezing the local planetary crust. This compression created central California's northwest-southeast-trending faults and rugged terrain, as some rocks between faults dropped to become valleys while others rose to become ridges and peaks. As mountains rose, erosion removed layers of sediment that had covered older rocks.

Mount Diablo itself began its rise above the surrounding Coast Range about five hundred thousand years ago. Faulting activity then began to create another of the mountain's surprises. A basic axiom of geology is that older rocks underlie younger ones, but Mount Diablo is an exception. Faulting there thrust Jurassic-period rocks over younger rock strata that had covered them for millions of years. Outcrops of such Jurassic igneous rocks—deep-ocean volcanics called pillow basalts—dot the summit today. A band of equally ancient material from earth's mantle, a slick blue-green rock called serpentine, runs along the north sides of the summit and North Peak. Most rocks on Diablo's middle slopes, by contrast, are metamorphosed sedimentary cherts and schists formed during the subsequent Cretaceous period, which ended 65 million years ago. In steep lower canyons, sedimentary outcrops such as Castle Rock's marine sandstones date from the Tertiary period, between 50 million and 10 million years ago. They're full of fossil oysters and snails. Younger Tertiary deposits containing bones of mastodons, camels, and other extinct mammals occur in the foothills.

Geologists do not understand exactly why Mount Diablo's older rocks have risen so far above the surrounding ridges' younger ones. One theory is that a particularly deep thrust fault underlies the peak at a depth so great (perhaps ten miles) that it is hard to detect. (Thrust faults are diagonal faults caused by the complex stresses of plate interaction.) This fault may have developed because the unusually massive chunk of Jurassic rock that includes the mountain's summit blocked two shallower faults, the Greenville on the southeast and the Concord on the northwest, from connecting across it. The blockage could have displaced the pressures that formed the shallower faults deeper into earth's crust, pushing the older rocks over the younger ones. Erosion would have removed the top of the up-thrust sheet, exposing the Jurassic rocks.

Deep thrust faults can hold enormous stress and are suspected of causing disastrous earthquakes, such as the 1994 Northridge Quake in Los Angeles. So, although it is not a volcano, Mount Diablo may yet be a source of geological upsets. Meanwhile, the summit continues to rise at a rate of about one to three millimeters a year.

AN ECOLOGICAL CROSSROADS

The plate tectonic theory of mountain origins is one of geology's great achievements. But that hasn't exhausted Mount Diablo's capacity for scientific surprises, which can concern very small things as well as very big ones. When William H. Brewer, Josiah Whitney's botanical assistant on the state geological survey, was exploring the mountain in May 1862, for example, he collected a pink annual wildflower that he evidently thought little of at the time. He didn't mention it in his notes, although the area where he found it, east of the peak, impressed him. He described it as "a flat of perhaps two or three hundred acres surrounded by low rolling hills and covered with oaks here and there, like a park. And such oaks! . . . one was seven feet in diameter, with a head a hundred and thirty feet across."

The wildflower, with spindly stems from four inches to two feet tall, would have seemed insignificant in comparison, and rather ordinary. It was a kind of *Eriogonum* (Latin for "wooly knees," referring to its cottony stems), a buckwheat-family genus of which the West has more than a hundred species. The little plant wasn't all that ordinary, as it happened. When Brewer sent his specimens east to Harvard, Asa Gray and Sereno Watson, two leading botanists, decided it was a new species, which they named *Eriogonum truncatum* in 1871. Even this wouldn't have surprised Brewer, who found other new species in California, then largely unexplored botanically. But as the state became better known, nobody found *E. truncatum* anywhere except Mount Diablo, and that might have surprised Brewer. The species, now called Mount Diablo buckwheat, seemed to be endemic to the area.

Such a discovery had important implications at a time when Darwin's theories were changing ideas about life's history. One implication was that the little plant might have come into existence fairly recently as evolution, through natural selection, led to "the origin of species." According to Darwinism, isolation from an original species would have caused Mount Diablo buckwheat to evolve new characteristics as it adapted to changing conditions. Brewer found it on dry sites, suggesting that it had adapted to the peak's lengthening rain shadow. Indeed, Mount Diablo turned out to be a major center of such plant endemism. At least another fourteen plant species (including a sunflower, a manzanita, and a globe lily) occur only in the area, suggesting that the new conditions caused by its relatively rapid rise over the past half million years have caused them to diverge from more common and widespread relatives.

"The native plants of California are some of the most exciting in the world," says botanist Peter Raven. "Many of them are of recent origin geologically, and the Mount Diablo buckwheat is clearly one of those." Yet *E. truncatum* is unusual even for a local endemic, because it is the mountain's most elusive one. After Brewer's discovery, it disappeared until 1886, when a botanist named Mary Katherine Curran identified it near Antioch, and then again until 1903, when another named C. F. Baker found it "locally common along rocky banks" on Marsh Creek Road east of the peak, near where Brewer had discovered it. Then nobody collected it again until the 1930s, when a young UC–Berkeley graduate student found some specimens.

That rediscovery would become part of a lifelong involvement with the mountain for that student, Mary Bowerman, although she would have been surprised if someone had told her so at the time. As she recalled, she "hadn't thought of Mount Diablo as being anything special" when her botany professor assigned her to study it in 1930. He chose her because she had a car. Yet Bowerman grew increasingly fascinated with the mountain as she explored it in the ensuing years, visiting it more than a hundred times and collecting many hundreds of plant species. In 1932 she surprised her thesis adviser, the eminent botanist Willis Lynn Jepson, by proposing to write her doctoral dissertation on the whole mountain's vegetation and its interactions with the physical environment. She proposed to approach the vegetation not just as an assemblage of plant species to be cataloged individually but as a system of plant communities, each with typical members and conditions. Such an ecological approach was relatively new at the time.

"During my studies, I became more interested in ecology than in straight identification," she wrote. "I kept track of which plants were growing together because it was so completely fresh to me. . . . I soon realized that Mount Diablo is a unique geographical location. It's part of the inner Coast Ranges yet is subject to coastal influence owing to the absence of high mountains to the west over the Bay. It's also a pivotal link between the differing vegetation units to the north and south Coast Ranges. The broad variations in temperature, rainfall, wind exposure, and altitude account for its wide variety of plant life." Bowerman completed her thesis in 1936. An expanded version, published in 1944 as *The Flowering Plants and Ferns of Mount Diablo, California,* is a major reference on the mountain's natural history.

The book takes an evolutionary as well as an ecological approach. Bowerman notes that the area's vegetation was very different before Mount Diablo arose. Fossils discovered nearby show that a forest of bald cypress and tupelo, trees like those now found in southeastern swamps, grew here in the Miocene epoch (23 to 5 million years ago). Some plants like those of that prehistoric forest—deciduous trees like box elder and sycamore—remained, but as the land gradually became drier and hillier, others moved in to create today's biotic mosaic.

Rising over the past five hundred thousand years, Mount Diablo became an ecological crossroads because of its central location and diverse topography. Organisms that occur north to British Columbia's rain forests intersect with ones that occur south to Mexico's deserts. Western pond turtles, red-legged frogs, and varied thrushes like those of Redwood National Park coexist with tarantulas, roadrunners, and western whiptail lizards like those of Joshua Tree National Park. On September evenings, when tarantulas roam in search of mates, the mountain is so dry that it might almost be desert. On nights in March, when red-legged frogs look for breeding pools, it can be so wet that it might almost be rain forest.

THE MOUNTAIN'S MOSAIC

Bowerman's book divides this biotic mosaic into plant communities based on the varied conditions. The riparian community, growing along streams in places like Sycamore and Curry Canyons, has deciduous trees such as alder, bigleaf maple, and cottonwood. Sun-dappled grapevines twine overhead, and shrubs like snowberry cover the ground. Almost as lush, but shadier, is the broadleaf sclerophyll community, which grows in moist places such as the north-facing slopes above Pine, Curry, and Mitchell Canyons. Most of its species, including coast live oak, madrone, and California laurel, have tough evergreen (sclerophyllous) leaves adapted to dry summers. The deciduous oak–pine community occurs on rockier, dryer areas such as Castle Rock and Rock City and also on ridgetops and flats, where scattered valley oak, blue oak, and black oak— mixed with ghost pines, Coulter pines, and knobcone pines—grow among grasses and wildflowers.

Bowerman's other two plant communities occur in places where trees have trouble growing. The grassland community gives the mountain its fireworks of poppies and lupines in spring and its golden glow in summer. Exotic weeds have severely impacted it, but native plants survive in many places on the mountain. On Long Ridge, serpentine soil discourages weeds, and native goldfields, tarweeds, and poppies still bloom thickly. Bald Ridge and Donner Canyon also have expanses of native grassland. The chaparral community occurs in places too dry, steep, and rocky even for grassland, covering most of the mountain's south-facing slopes with a shaggy carpet of shrubs that would be desert-like if it weren't so dense. Chaparral may look monotonous, but it has a special wealth of native shrubs and forbs. These flower throughout most of the year: manzanita in early winter, aromatic buckbrush in spring, chamise in the heat of summer. Chaparral flowers, from the white of chamise and buckbrush to the neon magenta of chaparral pea and the electric blue of California lilac, can be so profuse that they color entire slopes and perfume the air.

Even the mosaic of plant communities doesn't quite capture the complexity of the mountain's ecology. The transition zones between them form distinct habitats of their own. The elusive Mount Diablo buckwheat appears to depend on one such boundary habitat, between grassland and chaparral. C. F. Baker, the early plant collector, noted that the little plant grew in places where the two communities met, and that was where Mary Bowerman found it, growing with shrubs such as poison oak and California sagebrush but also with grasses such as brome.

That was significant, because many new species tend to evolve in such transition zones. So *E. truncatum* might well have evolved in the last half million years as the mountain's rising slopes and lengthening rain shadow created new conditions. But it was hard to learn more about the little wildflower because Bowerman didn't find any specimens after 1936; nor did anyone else. As decades passed, Mount Diablo buckwheat seemed to have died out.

THE COST OF GROWTH

Mount Diablo buckwheat's extinction would not have been a surprise in the twentieth century, given the human forces increasingly arrayed against rare organisms. While the native Bolbones had burned vegetation to foster food plants and game, that probably hadn't threatened annuals like *E. truncatum*. It may have benefited them by reducing competition from the perennial plants that dominated California's native grasslands. The advent of European agriculture changed things. Spanish livestock brought seeds of aggressive weeds such as wild oats, and heavy grazing allowed them to replace native grasses and forbs over large areas. Grazing intensified when Americans homesteaded the mountain. They also cut trees and burned chaparral to increase livestock yield and plowed flats for hay and other crops. Miners dug up hillsides in search of lime, coal, and mercury. The peak became a popular resort after the building of Mountain House Hotel just below the summit in the 1870s.

Although homesteads failed because of the semiarid climate, surrounding towns grew quickly and entrepreneurs looked to the mountain for more space. Between 1910 and 1917, a speculator named Robert Noble Burgess acquired some sixty square miles in the area, realigned old stagecoach roads for automobiles, and extended them to the summit. (These routes, which Burgess called the Mount Diablo Scenic Boulevard, would become the park's North Gate and South Gate Roads.) Burgess hoped to build a huge housing estate on his land, and he was not alone. In 1914, William Randolph Hearst, the newspaper magnate, contemplated buying fifteen thousand acres and placing a castle-like hotel on the summit.

Mount Diablo proved too remote and rugged, however. Hearst built his castle at San Simeon instead, and Burgess went bankrupt during World War I. Another entrepreneur, Walter P. Frick, continued to hold land on the mountain, and if the 1920s boom had continued, he might have subdivided much of it. Yet Frick liked the mountain's natural landscape (he let Mary Bowerman collect there), and the 1929 Wall Street collapse threatened his finances. By then, headlong growth had generated a movement to save open space with state parks, so Frick sold six parcels, a total of 2,004 acres, to the state. The first two of these were dedicated as Mount Diablo State Park in 1931.

Most of the mountain remained in private hands, subject to heavy grazing, quarrying, hunting, and other impacts. Increased pesticide use and poisoning of coyotes and ground squirrels threatened uncommon species like eagles, burrowing owls, falcons, kit foxes, and badgers. Although urban growth pressure remained comparatively light through World War II, this changed after construction of the Caldecott Tunnel. Freeways and suburbs devoured the valleys' fields and orchards, and as growth accelerated with the construction of BART in the 1970s, subdivisions spread into the canyons and foothills. Just one of these, Blackhawk Ranch at the foot of Sycamore Canyon west of the park, proposed to cover some forty-two hundred acres with luxury homes and malls. That was nearly as large as the state park itself, which had grown to 6,788 acres in the 1960s through state bond measures but which still excluded most of the mountain.

PROTECTING THE WHOLE

New factors began to resist wholesale urbanization at this point, and the last person to locate Mount Diablo buckwheat played a big part in that resistance. Over the years, Mary Bowerman's fascination with the mountain's natural habitats had generated a passion to protect them. She foresaw that a small park around the summit wouldn't do that in the long run. "Because there's so much variation between different parts of the mountain, we need preservation of the whole to understand the whole ecological picture," she wrote. "It is my dream that the whole of Mount Diablo, including its foothills, will remain open space."

Bowerman's concern for Mount Diablo's ecosystem was active as well as informed. She would surprise local landowners such as the Wright family—owners of a recreation park in Curry Canyon—by suddenly appearing and asking what could be done to preserve the mountain. "She was talking about us donating [land] when we were just starting to buy it," Dorothy Wright recalled. "We thought she was crazy, but she'd talk about nature, the future, the mountain, then five or six years later she'd show up again." Bowerman's persistence eventually paid off with Dorothy Wright, who sold part of her land for inclusion in the park in 2002. "I realize now," Wright said, "what a neat thing it is to have your priorities in something that will last into perpetuity."

Bowerman moved from Berkeley to Lafayette in 1954 and became active in local conservation groups. She found that Mount Diablo often took a backseat to other causes, however, so she started asking: "What can we do for the mountain right here?" In 1971, her concern prompted Art Bonwell, an engineer who liked to hike and bicycle in the park, to suggest that they start an organization dedicated to saving the whole mountain as open space. Bonwell had served as chair of the Sierra Club's Mount Diablo Regional Group and knew a lot of conservationists, so, as he said, "I was the organizer and she was the inspiration." Save Mount Diablo (SMD) held its first meeting in December of that year, with twenty participants chipping in twenty-five cents apiece to get the minutes mailed.

From the start, SMD advocated expanding the state park through public acquisitions. Thanks to a combination of citizen pressure and state park funds, the park had grown to more than nineteen thousand acres by 2000. When public bodies were short of money to buy important parcels that became available, SMD often raised the funds to acquire them for eventual transfer to public ownership. The first purchase was 117 acres at the corner of Marsh Creek and Morgan Territory Roads in 1976.

Conservation funds are always limited, and SMD developed other strategies to protect as much of the mountain as possible. It opposed subdivisions that encroached on significant natural habitats and tried to mitigate urbanization by encouraging owners to dedicate parts of their lands to conservation. An early example of this involved the huge Blackhawk Ranch proposal. In the 1970s, SMD negotiated for 2,052 of the property's 4,200 acres to be dedicated to the state park as a condition of building the subdivision. This acreage includes many of the most scenic areas on the mountain's southwest flank, such as the Black Hills, the Wall Point area, Blackhawk Ridge, and parts of Dan Cook and Jackass Canyons.

CONSERVATION CORRIDORS

As urbanization continued to spread, SMD and other conservationists saw that protecting Mount Diablo itself would not be enough to ensure long-term preservation of its biotic diversity. Studies of "island ecology" show that isolated natural areas steadily lose such diversity. Wild populations are always prone to local extinction under natural stress from predation, disease, and climate, but recolonization from adjacent areas replenishes them. When urbanization surrounds a park, natural flora and fauna may fail to renew depleted populations.

Mount Diablo has lost diversity in recent times. Native rainbow trout inhabited Mitchell Creek until the 1980s but haven't been found recently. Plant species have disappeared, and not just rare ones. Mary Bowerman found leopard lilies on the mountain in the 1930s, but the magnificent orange wildflowers have not been seen since, probably because of livestock trampling and browsing at springs.

Yet island ecology studies also show that relatively small areas can protect diverse animal and plant populations if they are linked to form "wildlife corridors" along which migration, recolonization, and other natural processes can continue. Since the park's founding, charismatic species like mountain lions and bobcats have persisted there because other, albeit still-unprotected natural areas border it. The future of diversity thus depends on establishing and maintaining wildlife corridors.

Accordingly, conservationists' primary objective shifted from expanding the state park to promoting open space corridors around the mountain, a timely move as urbanization threatened to isolate the park from vital areas that the East Bay Regional Park District (EBRPD) was acquiring—Morgan Territory to the east and Black Diamond Mines to the north. On the west slope, where urbanization pressure was strongest, SMD worked with EBRPD and local communities to protect open space around the park at Wall Ridge, Lime Ridge, Shell Ridge, Crystal Ranch, and other areas.

SMD's ultimate goal became linking Mount Diablo's nineteenth thousand plus acres with roughly ninety thousand acres of other protected open space outside the state park, from Walnut Creek and Antioch in the north to Livermore in the south. These forty or more separate open space units would not be isolated preserves but anchors for a 180,000-acre wilderness complex that would let plants and animals continue to circulate naturally. The concept of a Diablo Grand Loop embodies the goal: a continuous trail through the open space of the northern Diablo Range, from Mount Diablo south to the Los Vaqueros watershed, looping north and east through Cowell Ranch State Park and Black Diamond Mines Regional Preserve.

Once corridors are established, SMD's long-term strategy includes the restoration of native species like rainbow trout and leopard lilies. Successful restoration of peregrine falcons in the area in the 1990s was an encouraging sign. Conservationists hope that the California condor may return to forage or even nest on Mount Diablo someday. With enough protection, some apparently vanished species may also "restore" themselves. A particularly encouraging example of this happened recently.

RETURN OF A NATIVE

Mary Bowerman died in August 2005, but not before her life's work took a surprising turn. Her book, *The Flowering Plants and Ferns of Mount Diablo*, went out of print in the mid-1990s, so she began collaborating with Barbara Erter, a botanist at UC–Berkeley's Jepson Herbarium, on an updated version (published by the California Native Plant Society in 2002). The project involved intensive new exploration of the mountain's vegetation, and collectors found a number of plants as yet not recorded there, although they failed to find some recorded ones, including Mount Diablo buckwheat.

Exploration continued after the book's publication, and in May 2005, a UC–Berkeley graduate student happened on a little pink annual wildflower growing between grassland and chaparral. "I was looking at a common plant that likes rock outcroppings and wondering why it was growing on sand," recalled the student, Michael Park, "when I realized that I was surrounded by early blooming buckwheat. I decided I needed a closer look since I didn't recognize it and then I realized this was something new."

Park was looking at a species that no one had collected for seven decades—*Eriogonum truncatum*. "Once I knew it was Mount Diablo buckwheat," he said, "I was in shock. . . . It's a surprisingly dainty plant once you see it in the field, because it's so celebrated in the botanical community that it had grown in my imagination. It's only because I stopped and was moving more slowly that I realized it was there."

Barbara Erter and other botanists confirmed Park's identification of the plant. By chance, news of a possible sighting in Arkansas of an ivory-billed woodpecker—also considered extinct for decades—had emerged three weeks earlier, so the media was primed to notice returns from apparent oblivion. National Public Radio interviewed Erter and Seth Adams, SMD's land programs director, who exulted: "With all the normal controversies and lands battles, what great news that this beautiful and unique wildflower has managed to survive. When I visited the site, I was struck by how fragile the plant is. There are fewer than twenty, it's an annual and reseeds and dies each year, but it has survived."

The species's future remains uncertain, in part because botanists aren't sure *how* it has managed to survive. One theory involves brush rabbits, which hide from predators in dense chaparral and venture into adjacent grassland to feed. By thinning exotic weeds at the chaparral's edge, the rabbits may benefit the rare native annual. But science still knows little about protecting endangered species like Mount Diablo buckwheat. Propagating them in nurseries can preserve their genetic material—botanists at UC–Berkeley Botanical Garden grew the species from seeds collected in 2005—but organisms can't really survive unless viable populations continue to reproduce in their natural habitats. The plant's reappearance on the mountain in the following year was good news, but no guarantee of ultimate survival.

It kept coming back to preserving habitat. "Our first priority," said SMD executive director Ron Brown, "is to make sure that Mount Diablo is not cut off from the rest of the Diablo Range to the south, so that the area retains healthy breeding populations and an enriched gene pool of plants and animals. Second, although SMD has done a good job of defining the outer edges of the habitat we want to protect, we need to fill in those limits with large enough swaths of protected land to sustain wildlife and provide visual and recreational amenities."

Brown said that SMD has benefited from good relations with landowners who share its values and goals. An example of this is the 2006 purchase of the Mangini Ranch at the park's northwest side, a crucial acquisition, facilitated by a State Coastal Conservancy grant, that links the park with Walnut Creek's Lime Ridge Open Space. The 208-acre ranch, in the Mangini family for more than 125 years, has exceptional habitat for wildlife and plants, including the northernmost stand of desert olive, a typical Mojave Desert shrub, and several endemic wildflowers such as hospital canyon larkspur, a pink-flowered species that stands up to six feet tall in wet years. It is one of the sites where Mary Bowerman found Mount Diablo buckwheat, and although the plant has not surfaced there since, its grassland–chaparral interface habitat remains.

"We believe that our ancestors would be very proud of us for working with Save Mount Diablo," said Karen Mangini, one of the ranch's owners. "It is our responsibility to protect this land for others. We want future generations to enjoy what we had; we want them to be able to roam among the land's friendly confines as we have done. We hope that the work we are doing with Save Mount Diablo will encourage other farming and ranching families in this beautiful valley to do likewise."

SMD estimated at that time that the amount of protected land in the area would have to double before its work was finished, quite a challenge. California didn't pass a major park bond issue between Proposition 70 in 1988 and Propositions 12 and 40 in 2000 and 2002. Those funds were soon spent. Land prices were jumping dramatically, and the state was having trouble managing its existing parks, let alone expanding the system. "Urban pressure for large scale developments in the foothills has never been greater," said former SMD board president Bob Doyle.

But Mount Diablo continues to specialize in surprises, as I found when I visited a place near where William Brewer first found *Eriogonum truncatum.* Round Valley Regional Preserve is in the peak's rain shadow to the southeast of the state park and has desert species like kit foxes and roadrunners, so I'd anticipated a forbidding, even infernal place. But it was a wet April, and it was more like *Fantasia*'s bucolic "Pastoral Symphony" sequence than its diabolic "Night on Bald Mountain." Meadowlarks sang in buttercup-spangled turf; bluebirds, goldfinches, and warblers thronged oaks rivaling those that Brewer described in 1861.

I didn't find Mount Diablo buckwheat, but I did find something unexpected. When the Lewis and Clark expedition was exploring the West in 1805, they discovered a large species of woodpecker with plumage unlike that of any other in the United States. Its back and wings were a dark, glossy green, and Captain Meriwether Lewis described its breast plumage as "a curious mixture of white and blood red which has the appearance of having been artificially stained that color." The species's behavior was unusual too: it flew straight ahead like a crow (most woodpeckers have an arcing flight) and hawked insects from a perch. Since Lewis was the first to describe it, taxonomists named it after him.

Looking up to Round Valley's foothill oak woodlands, I saw a nearly crow-sized bird flying straight through the trees and perching to hawk insects from them. When I got near enough, I saw that it had a green back and pink breast. It was a Lewis's woodpecker, the first I'd seen in decades of hiking the Bay Area. Like Mount Diablo buckwheat, the species has specialized habitat needs—expanses of parklike savanna—and faces threats from exotic species and human activities. Starlings preempt its nest holes in savanna trees, and logging, overgrazing, and development threaten savanna. Round Valley almost became a landfill before EBRPD acquired it. If it had, I would not have seen the species near the peak.

My favorite Mount Diablo surprise so far was in the park itself, on rocky, windswept Eagle Peak Trail one hot May morning. An exuberant end-of-term school hike had started from the Mitchell Canyon area that day, so I thought wildlife would be scarce along the trails. As I walked through thick old chaparral on a saddle north of Eagle Peak, however, the pebbly red soil coalesced into a creature that had seemed almost mythical because I'd often heard of it but had never seen it—a coast horned lizard. It was a large stout specimen, but it blended so well with the ground that I probably would have missed it if I'd been in a hurry. Mary Austin describes the spooky camouflage of its smaller, more common desert relative in her classic *The Land of Little Rain*: "Now and then a palm's breadth of trail gathers itself and scurries off with a rustle under the brush, to resolve itself into sand again. This is pure witchcraft."

This horned lizard had even more confidence in witchcraft than its desert relative—it just stayed on the trail. As I sat down and watched it for a half hour, it moved twice—once to blink an eye, once to move a foot. Only when I had crept up close enough to touch it did it scurry off, and then it just disguised itself as pebbly red dirt again a little way within the chaparral. Its behavior was fascinating if also troubling given the species's evident scarcity in the park. Mountain bicyclists had left many tracks on the legally off-limits hiking trail. That lizard would have had no chance to "scurry off with a rustle" if one had come along.

Enough range and habitat for Lewis's woodpeckers and coast horned lizards exist outside the crowded Bay Area that neither species is endangered. Lewis's woodpeckers live from central British Columbia to northern Mexico and east to the Great Plains; coast horned lizards from the northern Sacramento Valley to Baja California. It's still a thrill to see them here. Such sightings show that the biodiversity protection strategy of Save Mount Diablo and its allies is working. The more linked habitat there is in the area, the more chance there is that a Lewis's woodpecker, a coast horned lizard, or even a Mount Diablo buckwheat will be here to surprise us.

—*Bay Nature*, July–September 2006

beavers and boutiques

I had heard so much about the beavers that colonized downtown Martinez in 2006 that I thought they would be easy to find. A brief Internet search disclosed no directions or maps, however. I set out anyway and eventually found myself in Martinez, although on the way I didn't see any billboards welcoming me to the Bay Area's beaver capital. The downtown also offered a conspicuous absence of signage. Yet it was in fact easy to find the beaver colony.

A line of willows and cottonwoods, the borders of Alhambra Creek, snaked through the restaurants and shops, and although beaver signage was absent, beaver word of mouth wasn't. The first passerby I asked knew when and where to find them and directed me to three dams downstream from where I was on Main Street. Heading that way, I could see that it was an unusual downtown. Large turtles swam in the creek, and even more unusual, baby turtles did too. Mallards and snowy egrets appeared, which was not so unusual, but the sight of a pair of green herons was. Green herons need riparian woodland, scarce along diverted and culverted California streams. I heard they'd been absent from Alhambra Creek before the beavers arrived.

When I came to the dams, it was something of an anticlimax. Compared to a lot of beaver dams, they weren't very impressive—and beaver dams can be very impressive indeed, as can their other engineering works. On a trek into Montana's Beartooth-Absaroka Wilderness in 1978, they'd astonished and mystified me. I was used to low dams across gentle eastern streams, but the Montana beavers had adapted their work to rugged terrain along what is called, not too accurately, the Stillwater River. When I passed the steep ravine of a river tributary, it looked as though Asian rice farmers had terraced it. A series of check dams ran up as far as I could see, turning what must have been a torrent into a string of quiet ponds. Some of the dams were considerably taller than me, with arching shapes so regular and elegant that they resembled miniature Grand Coulees.

I knew they were beaver dams, since they consisted of gnawed branches. That wasn't true of another engineering feat I saw there. In a large marsh on the river, I found a canal that cut through the rushes and sedges with such straightness and precision—the spoil piled neatly along the banks—that the Army Corps of Engineers seemed the likely agent, although this was a day's walk from the nearest road. Reading up on beavers, however, I found that they often dig canals, even more impressive ones. They dig ones as much as one thousand feet long to divert streams into home ponds or to reach food sources. (They prefer herbaceous marsh plants like cattails but also eat the inner bark of trees like willows and cottonwoods, partly because branches can be stored underwater when ponds are frozen in winter.) If the canals pass through sloping terrain, moreover, they build small check dams at intervals along them so that the water won't flow too fast.

The abundance of such feats in North American beaver colonies amazed Europeans (who already had decimated Old World beavers for the fur trade), although early accounts tended to exaggerate. On the eve of the American Revolution, a Captain John Carver described how, "after mature deliberation," troops of two or three hundred beavers assembled to build dams; how they plastered the dams with "a kind of mortar . . . laid on with their tails"; and how they built their "cabins . . . on poles." Illustrations showed beaver lodges with square, framed windows and second stories. Alexander Majors, originator of the Pony Express, said that beavers "had more engineering skill than the entire Corps of Engineers who were connected with General Grant's army when he besieged Vicksburg."

The size, complexity, and skill of beaver colonies really are amazing, and they became prime subjects for an "instinct versus intelligence" controversy that agitated the emerging sciences of biology and psychology in the nineteenth century. Traditional lore had granted nonhuman animals a degree of reasoning power, to the extent that they sometimes were tried and punished for crimes. This went against the Judeo-Christian doctrine that they lack souls, however, and eighteenth-century Enlightenment-era science, influenced by Cartesian mechanistic dualism, tended to dismiss such lore. Frederic Cuvier, head keeper of the Paris zoo and younger brother of the early-nineteenth-century's most famous naturalist, Baron Georges Cuvier, set out to test the question by raising a pair of beaver kits in isolation. The pair cut down trees and built dams with the branches, thus demonstrating, he thought, all the talents and abilities of wild beavers. He decided that their behavior was purely instinctive.

Yet Cuvier's experiment was inconclusive because naturalists had not really studied beavers in the wild. The fur industry kept well ahead of them, exterminating colonies as they became accessible. In California, trappers wiped out one of the continent's largest beaver populations even before the gold rush, decimating Native Americans with Old World diseases in the process. They wiped out beavers so fast, indeed, that it's unclear just what their role in the Bay Area's ecology was. Although early accounts mention beavers throughout the area, biologists assume they mainly lived in the delta, with its abundant water supply. Many Bay Area creeks ran all year then, however, so the early accounts of beavers all around the Bay may have something. (Early accounts described sea otters throughout the Bay, which seems strange now.)

I remember my surprise, after hiking down a Maryland creek that empties into Chesapeake Bay, at finding a large beaver pond (more of a lake, really) right by the bay's shore. There were dams upstream too, predictably, but beaver coastal engineering seemed counterintuitive. There it was though. It made me wonder what role beavers might have played in forming the San Francisco Bay marshes.

The fur industry expected to keep "harvesting" beavers until it exterminated them, as it apparently exterminated sea otters and fur seals. But the big rodents proved too widespread and resilient. Small colonies survived and recovered after the industry collapsed, with some help from conservationists. Industrious and familial, beavers underwent a late-nineteenth-century vogue, perhaps comparable to dolphins' late-twentieth-century one. Naturalists who studied them then weren't at all sure that their activities were purely instinctive.

Canals seemed the most striking suggestion of beaver intelligence because they implied planning. One naturalist, Alexander Dugmore, noted that when beavers built a canal toward a grove of food trees, they dug it before they cut the trees, not while they were moving back and forth to cut them. They apparently dug it with the conscious intention of providing access to a planned "timber sale." Another naturalist, Enos Mills, thought beaver "logging" also showed foresight:

"He occasionally endeavors to fell trees in a given direction," Mills wrote. "He avoids cutting those entangled at the top. . . . Sometimes he will, on a windy day, fell trees on the windward side of a grove . . . he commonly avoids felling trees in the heart of the grove, but cuts on the outskirts of it." Mills found that beavers generally took good care of their dams and lodges, plastering them with mud and promptly repairing damage. They sometimes built lodges over springs, which eliminated the danger of water freezing around the entrance in winter, trapping the occupants inside.

When I was in Montana in midsummer 1978, a large lodge in the ravine that beavers had terraced so impressively wasn't even in water at the time. It loomed by the creek bank like an untidy wooden castle. It didn't have windows, but it was tall enough for two beaver-sized stories. Apparently it was a seasonal residence to occupy when the stream level was higher from fall to spring.

Mills also saw beavers display the reverse of foresight, cutting trees that were entangled with others or located in the middle of a grove and thus impossible to move. He found dead beavers that had felled trees on themselves. Some beavers, especially young and solitary ones, were sloppy or perfunctory dam builders. They might build dams needlessly, as when transplanted to an already existing beaver pond. But individual idiocy doesn't prove general stupidity—otherwise *Homo sapiens* will have to change its name. Individual beavers' brilliance or incompetence could also imply that their engineering involves thinking as well as instinct.

But if a beaver thinks, how does it think? Humans largely think through language: we don't build dams or canals without it. Beavers are quiet creatures, although they do make various communicative noises, including the well-known tail slap on the water. But such noises don't seem complex enough to expound engineering techniques. Young beavers' sloppy dam construction suggests that parents pass on expertise, but the kits may simply learn through observation instead of instruction. Mills saw little evidence of leadership in groups of beavers at work, although he noted one instance wherein parents accompanied their young to a new location, helped them build a dam and lodge, and then returned to their old pond, leaving the youngsters at the new one.

Given the intelligence question's continuing relevance, the beavers' colonization of downtown Martinez in 2006 might be an extension of Frederic Cuvier's original experiment, albeit under reverse circumstances. Instead of Cuvier's naive beaver kits, observed in the zoo's protected environment, the Martinez "experiment" took a pair of mature, presumably experienced beavers and placed them in an environment that was very dangerous for beavers.

The experiment might have seemed conclusive enough if the Martinez authorities had killed the beaver pair that dammed Alhambra Creek, as they meant to do. (Authorities routinely kill beavers when their engineering might interfere with urban growth or agribusiness.) That would have tended to support Cuvier. Although the offending pair's origins are unclear, they presumably came from a more beaver-friendly habitat, some less urbanized wetland or stream. Foresight might have told them that a busy downtown was a problematic place for a dam. Beavers don't have to build dams: they can live in stream-bank dens instead of stick-and-mud lodges in dammed ponds. Damming a creek bordered by multistory buildings might well seem a thoughtlessly destructive product of blind instinct.

On the other hand, killing the subject of a behavioral experiment when some desired conclusion is reached has a way of biasing the experiment. As it happened, the intervention of local environmentalists, who formed a beaver protection organization, Worth A Dam, prevented the pair's immediate execution. So the experiment continued, with more problematic results.

The dam didn't flood the downtown during the next eight years. This probably was at least partly because Worth A Dam installed a control device in it to keep the water below a certain level. Yet the beavers' failure to flood the town also raised the possibility that their behavior might have been less unreasonable than it seemed, at least from a beaver's viewpoint. Beavers dam streams because they need water to swim in, and they can build very large ones to make very large ponds. The rudimentary nature of the Martinez dams could imply that the beavers were not simply damming blindly away but were engineering in proportion to an environment to which they perceived limits. Flooding buildings (perhaps perceived as cliff-like structures) would not turn them into beaver ponds, so why flood them?

The beavers' survival and reproduction in downtown Martinez might thus suggest some kind of reasoned adjustment to environment. The original dam's rudimentary size could have been simply a result of just two beavers working on it, but the dam didn't get bigger when the beavers had young, although they did build two more dams downstream, perhaps in reaction to increased water velocity caused by the control device on the first dam. Those two dams are also unimpressive. As to other activities, I thought I saw evidence of canal building in a marshy area beside the lower dams, probably to reach patches of cattails, but it also seemed rudimentary. The beavers didn't seem to have tried building lodges—they lived in bank burrows. The passerby who told me where to find the dams had never heard of beaver lodges.

Of course, the beavers' failure to flood the downtown for eight years doesn't guarantee they won't help to flood it sometime, although Bay Area downtowns untroubled by beavers flood often enough. Antibeaver officials say the rodents destroyed thousands of dollars worth of flood-control improvements, such as tree plantings, although I didn't perceive anything on my visit except a dying, beaver-gnawed cottonwood. Willows, the main beaver food trees in the area, seemed abundant. Worth A Dam maintained that beavers were getting a relatively small proportion of their food from trees, since marsh plants were available.

At present, the Martinez experiment seems little more conclusive as to the intelligence versus instinct question than the Cuvier one, and for the same reason: we just don't know enough about the question. Indeed, we probably know less than we thought we did in the early nineteenth century. It was easier to define intelligence and instinct when naturalists like Frederic Cuvier believed a creator had imbued humans with unique reasoning powers that set them apart from other creatures. But two centuries of evolutionary biology have made such beliefs increasingly hard for scientists to hold, although most Americans, perhaps including Martinez officials, still hold them.

The scientific evidence suggests that the human mind evolved from the minds of earlier animals—that thinking is not an absolute phenomenon but a contingent and relative one that combines conscious "intelligence" with unconscious "instinct" in highly unpredictable and sometimes mindlessly destructive ways. Human intelligence is very well developed, of course, which makes our bouts of mindless destructiveness very impressive.

Whatever happens on Alhambra Creek, beavers probably won't ruin downtown Martinez. Given our historical background, humans probably will, somehow, sooner or later.

—2014

the south bay

sunol falcon watch

Falcons inspire almost universal admiration. Literatures around the world praise them. They are beautiful; fly faster than almost anything alive; and can be trained to catch ducks, pigeons, and other things people like to eat. Medieval noblemen went everywhere with theirs and amused themselves at banquets by setting their pets after blackbird flocks released from ornamental pies—thus the nursery rhyme.

It is ironic if not surprising that one of the most admired of birds has become one of the most threatened. Wild falcons are worth thousands to oil sheiks, who have depleted their native populations and now have the birds smuggled from Alaska. But falcons weren't of value to the pesticide manufacturers and farmers whose activities rendered their eggshells too thin for successful brooding in the 1950s. The most popular species, the peregrine falcon, which nested in the Palisades across the Hudson from New York City until the 1940s, was virtually extinct as a breeding bird in the contiguous United States by the 1970s.

The western United States was lucky enough to still have a breeding population of another species, the prairie falcon. Slightly smaller than the peregrine, it resides in remote areas with relatively low pesticide levels instead of migrating through urban and agribusiness land like the peregrine. Falconers considered it a substitute for peregrines, however, and they probably outnumbered the falcons. Some pairs hatched clutches for years only to have falconers steal them. Audubon societies and other conservation groups started setting round-the-clock guards on falcon nests during breeding season.

I volunteered to guard a prairie falcon nest in Sunol Regional Park for five days in 1974 and kept a journal that gives an account of some spring days in the California Coast Range. Less comfortably for me, it also gives an account of the kind of feckless human behavior that makes life harder for things like falcons. I'm not sure the prairie falcons were too fortunate in having me to guard them.

Did the falcon guard stay at his post, day after day, scanning the horizon for falcon thieves? Or was he drawn with rationalizations and self-justifications to spying on the falcons he was supposed to guard? At least he didn't climb down the cliff to photograph the fledglings in the nest as some guards reputedly did, and the fledglings were still there after he'd gone.

. . .

APRIL 28: When I arrive, two fence lizards are stretched out on top of the tent, one atop the other. The top lizard jumps off as I approach and starts to flee, then circles back. The bottom lizard merely cocks its head at me. I see the sun reflected in its eye. The day is dry and hot, although the hills are lush green. I put my gear in the tent and walk out to the cliff top. Hordes of swifts and swallows circle overhead as though jet-propelled. They seem to enjoy veering away from obstacles like my head at the last moment. One of the falcons appears suddenly in the air below me, screams, and swoops away.

I have to walk a mile to a well at an old barn for water. I go at sunset, when the hillsides are orange with the last light. Poorwills start to call in the canyons. A horned lark springs into the air beside the road and spirals upward, singing. When I get back to the tent, it's dark. Toads patrol sedately, beige colored, their pearl gray warts tipped with pale orange. They match the stones here, which are coated with gray-and-orange lichens.

I walk along the cliff top in the darkness. Some large bird flies up behind me silently—then shrieks. A moment later, when my heart stops racing, I glimpse it gliding down the gully at the other side of the cliff top, emitting a squeaky, three-note call. It is too stubby and shaggy to be a falcon. The cliff has a nocturnal nester, as I'll see.

· · ·

APRIL 29: In the first sunlight, strands of spider silk on the trees sparkle prismatic red, green, and blue. A meadowlark flies by with an earwig in its beak. Flocks of blackbirds pass overhead. In the gully's oak woods, Steller's jays search the trunks for insects. One jay circles me curiously, challenges my presence by imitating a red-tailed hawk scream, and then loses interest.

When I walk to the cliff top, a falcon drops off the nest (which is hidden by a rock overhang) and flies away along the spine of the ridge. I keep away from the edge after that. I never get a really close look at the birds or see the nest—that's not what I'm here for, after all. I content myself with observing the adults through binoculars.

Other inhabitants are less timid than the falcons. California ground squirrels from burrows around the tent are quite bold, casually, since my food doesn't interest them. As I eat lunch, one browses on yellow-flowered owl clover and pink-flowered filaree almost at my feet.

The cliff's daytime nesters include turkey vultures, and the big birds come and go frequently. The falcons stoop at them, a touchiness that might indicate that their eggs have hatched. The vultures just drop down a few feet—shrugging off the falcons' testiness—then fly on. Instead of returning to the nest after diving at the vultures, the falcons often plunge across the canyon and start a series of upward spirals that carry them out of sight.

It gets very hot, and I walk down into the gully. The live oaks' shade is cool and drowsy, very different from the windy, bustling cliff top. Lark sparrows—big handsome birds with chestnut brown markings— loiter around a half-dried stock pond. Male fence lizards chase up and down a buckeye trunk, pausing to puff up their throats and do "push ups," which flash azure scales on their flanks to attract females and discourage rivals. When they stop moving, their gray scales conceal them against the bark. Most animals are camouflaged here: the toads, the grasshoppers, which are either gray like pebbles or striped green and beige like grasses.

When I go to get water at sunset, a deer herd silhouetted against a ridgetop doesn't see me against the dark ground, so I get quite close before they bolt. The last to disappear is a well-antlered buck that seems to pose self-consciously against the pale sky. When the stars come out, coyotes call briefly from the eastern hills. After I get into my sleeping bag, a big black ground beetle keeps me awake by crawling around the tent.

. . .

APRIL 30: The wind has shifted to the west and the air is clammy with fog, which shrouds the canyons to the east. I get up late. A female oriole is trying to pull off some twine tied on a buckeye branch by the tent. The black-and-orange bird yanks at it from various angles and tries to fly away with it, but it keeps pulling her up short. She chatters irritably but keeps pulling at it for most of the morning, although it won't break. I finally cut off a piece and offer it to her, but she flees in terror. Soon she is back, tugging at the attached string while my offering dangles in the breeze.

Two ground squirrels frequent this place, an old one and a young one. The old one is bolder, the big-eyed youngster more curious. It spends a lot of time sniffing around the tent as I eat lunch.

I spy on the falcons from the ridgetop north of the cliff in the afternoon. When I get up to leave, a falcon flies quietly out of the trees behind my vantage point and swoops off down the gully. As I walk back past the cliff top, it returns and circles me watchfully.

Toward sunset, vultures perch on a dead tree across the gully and spread their wings to catch the last light slanting through the haze. A mourning dove calls. The wind rises and it gets chilly. At night I hear a bird scream, and, later on, gunfire.

. . .

MAY 1: I have bad dreams and wake up early. The fog is up to the cliff top, heavy and cold. I glimpse a falcon coursing along a ridgetop, looking for unwary meadowlarks. To get warm, I walk farther down the gully than previously. The woods are denser down there. A gray squirrel climbs slowly along an oak bough, pausing to scratch or nibble a young leaf. A red-tailed hawk or Steller's jay screams farther downhill. The grass is full of fairy lanterns, golden lily relatives named for their resemblance to Japanese paper lights.

The fog burns off in late morning. The ground squirrels emerge from their burrows, followed a little later by a toad. As it suns at the burrow entrance, the toad's orange markings look paler than they seemed at night in my flashlight beam. In the afternoon, one of the falcons brings a catch to the nest, a blackbird. The wind rises again, stronger than yesterday, and tosses the grass around the rocks.

When I go for water at sunset, I encounter a cattle herd near a burned ranch house, attended by starlings, blackbirds, and magpies. The cows regard me solemnly, except for two yearlings that stop butting each other and rush toward me, perhaps looking for something new to butt. I tell them to leave me alone, and they withdraw, but they soon turn back for another try, along with a cow and calf that are caught up in the excitement. I'm past the herd, however, and they lose interest. When I look back, one of the yearlings is trying to start a butting contest with the calf.

It's dark by the time I fill my canteens. The canyon beyond the barn looks spooky—it's full of pallid, wraith-like sycamores. The old windmill still creaks and splashes, although the ranch is abandoned—pumping water for animals and for the nettles and yellow monkey flowers clustered around its outflow. On the way back, a pair of green eyes streaks across the road in my flashlight beam, probably a coyote, since it runs level instead of bounding like a bobcat.

• • •

MAY 2: I've tried to resist an urge to see what is visible from the cliff bottom, but curiosity gets the best of me. I walk north along the ridge to a grassy hillside and descend to a buckeye thicket about a hundred feet below the foot of the cliff. Undeceived, a falcon watches me from the cliff crevice that probably contains its nest. A ground squirrel runs along the cliff face just above the crevice, but the falcon ignores it. When I enter the thicket, the falcon leaves its perch and dives down the canyon, a straight, steep dive that takes it out of sight.

I train my binoculars on the cliff. There are swallow nests on it—mud balls in rocky angles. About halfway down the cliff is a long, low fissure into which, it seems, someone has placed three upright rocks. I look more closely and see that they aren't rocks. A great horned owl and two owlets gaze down at me. The owl was probably what startled me on the cliff top my first night. The owlets look like gray velvet bolsters on which tiny white faces have been painted. Somehow I know they see me, despite my concealment in the thicket, although I can't see them without my binoculars. Their postures seem to register my every movement.

The vultures are sunning at the edge of their nest fissure, a more pala-tial one than the owls', which look like peas in a pod by comparison. Feral Eurasian rock doves flutter around their own nests in the cliffs, seeming much wilder than they do in town. None have the white plumage patches that mark their urban relatives—the raptors must see to that.

I climb back up the hillside through tall grass thick with California poppies, a perfect place for bees. Their buzzing is pervasive. It's not an entirely perfect place, however. About one poppy in ten conceals a yellow crab spider, its claws poised to grab unwary bees. Dry bee car-casses lie under the poppy stamens, the black-and-yellow stripes on their abdomens still bright.

When I reach the ridgetop, I meet a western whiptail lizard, a species that mainly inhabits desert, so it is a surprise among all the greenery. It is so intent on sunbathing that it lets me touch its back before it disappears in the lush grass.

It's windy again in the afternoon. A golden eagle (an immature one, its wings and tail marked with white) flies up the valley. Cattle start to bawl, which attracts vultures. Ten of them start circling the herd, first skimming close over it, then landing on rocks in a ring around it. They jockey for position, dominant birds lunging at timid ones. But the cows are unhurt, and the vultures depart. Meanwhile, a kestrel (a small falcon relative) has been loitering around the canyon, which eventually provokes a falcon to leave the nest and stoop at it. The kestrel flees, the falcon in pursuit.

I go for water late, after sundown. In the barn, a dead flicker hangs from the loft door, its foot caught in a crack. It looks so gruesome that I try to knock it down with rocks, but it is too dark to see.

As I'm getting into my sleeping bag, a toad hops into the tent. I wouldn't mind the company but I'm afraid of crushing it in my sleep, so I evict it. The indignity causes it to urinate on my hand, and I wonder where it gets the water on this dry cliff top. It's very cold tonight. The toad may have been attracted by the Coleman lantern's warmth.

· · ·

MAY 3: This is my last day. I haven't encountered any nest robbers, but they usually come on weekends. The guards I replaced turned away two teenagers with ropes and gauntlets who wanted to "just look" at the nest.

In the early morning I see deer across the gully, perhaps the herd I saw on the second day. They see me and imperceptibly work their way downhill out of sight. When the sun hits the treetops, they're gone. I find fresh coyote tracks in the mud around the stock pond when I walk down the gully.

Around noon, I hear someone on a hilltop to the east shouting: "I am God! I am God!" Otherwise, it's an uneventful day. The falcons fly back and forth to the nest and chase the vultures; the sun shines; the wind blows.

My skin has darkened, but I still feel as though I'm being broiled alive if I stay out of the shade very long. This is not really a place for human beings. At five, the truck brings my replacement and takes me away.

—*Berkeley Monthly*, April 1979

puddles

Coyote Hills Regional Park is a good place for one of the Bay Area's less appreciated features—rainy-season puddles. On a post-storm visit last winter, I walked through or around grassy sheets of water that covered most of the trail as I headed toward some Ohlone Indian mounds. The soggy landscape seemed empty at first, except for a black-shouldered kite on a fence post, but my passage scared a surprising number of birds from a willow-bordered slough—an American egret, a cinnamon teal flock, a black-crowned night heron, a mallard pair. Attracted by the commotion, a marsh harrier skimmed over, scaring out some coots and a pied-billed grebe.

Near the mounds, the trail became a temporary stream instead of a chain of puddles, so I stopped, enjoying the sunlight and looking into the puddles. There was a lot to see. What seemed at first glance to be just drowned mud and grass teemed with rapidly revolving greenish specks—untold numbers of small crustaceans—copepods, ostracods, and amphipods that spend the dry season as eggs in the soil, then hatch with the rains so they can mate and lay eggs to await the next rains. Here and there larger red specks pursued or clutched the green ones. These were mites, tiny spider relatives.

Less numerous than the specks, fortunately, were mosquito and gnat larvae, also called wrigglers because they move through the water by undulating their cylindrical bodies. Many other creatures—probably water beetles and bugs—swam or hid so energetically that I couldn't identify them. Every puddle I looked into had its population of revolving crustaceans, predacious mites, undulating fly larvae, and hyperactive beetle-bugs. It seemed primordial. The entire terrestrial planet must have been like it when life first spread out of the oceans: land's first inhabitants probably were tiny dwellers of puddles. I don't suppose the ones that stayed in them have changed much since. For an ostracod, a crustacean that lives in a translucent bivalved shell, the Paleozoic era has never ended.

Of course, other life has moved on, as proclaimed by cock pheasants that flew metallically squawking over my head every few minutes. A squeaky bubbling sound with angry overtones came from a patch of cattails, a racket so noisy that I was surprised when the caller finally hopped into sight. I'd thought it might be a rail, a good-sized wading bird, but it was a long-billed marsh wren, a small brown songbird that also lives only in marshes and so isn't heard much in the well-drained Bay Area. The wren flew into another patch of cattails, startling out a yellowthroat, a bright yellow warbler with a black mask.

I gave up on the inundated mounds and walked south across more semiflooded land that had been in crops before the park. An egret stood meditatively in the grass watching for voles, killdeer flocks called mournfully, and western chorus frogs began to croak in ditches and large puddles as the sun headed west. I almost stepped on a hen pheasant in a patch of burdock and sow thistle. The next field contained half a dozen ground squirrels, two jackrabbits, and shorebirds—sandpipers, willets, and avocets. The reddening sunlight made the black-and-white avocets look very showy against the green new grass and yellow mustard flowers.

The frog song rose to a syncopated din after sunset. Gray shapes like giant owls flew out of the dusk and landed in the fields—night herons from the willow thickets. Egrets and blue herons joined them, all hunting frogs and mice, all drifting aside like melancholy ghosts as I passed.

It was quite a spectacle, in an understated way, and I had it to myself. There were many visitors in the park, escaping after a stormy week indoors, but they stayed on the hills or on a boardwalk that ran through a permanent marsh west of the Ohlone mounds. The wet fields weren't an attraction, which seemed paradoxical given modern attitudes to natural areas. We value rarity, and little is rarer in the Bay Area than a bit of flat land that doesn't have buildings, agribusiness, or at least a duck marsh on it. But just flat land by itself doesn't have much appeal.

It wasn't always like that. Seventeenth- and eighteenth-century landscape paintings celebrate flatlands, although there's usually some pretext of farming or other useful practices going on there—cows, woodcutters.

The artists clearly have a strong feeling for the level meeting of earth and sky, however—clouds, water, bird flocks. But twentieth-century aesthetics seem to have erased this realm of landscape appreciation, at least in California.

I learned to love flatlands while working at a regional park agency in central Ohio, where they are nearly the only lands to love. Walking through the woods one warm March day, I idly peered into clear rivulets of snowmelt and began to see surprising things. Twigs and clots of sand crawled across the bottom. They were caddis fly larvae, insects that cement tubes of detritus with a sticky secretion and live in them. Grayish white specks that swam about kept changing shape unexpectedly—thin to fat and back to thin again. I scooped some up and saw that they were planarians, the droll, arrow-shaped flatworms featured in every biology textbook. Wild planarians! Soon I found another textbook mainstay, a hydra, a jellyfish relative that plants itself on sunken twigs like a tiny tree and snares passing crustaceans in its tentacles.

The snowmelt rivulets were like tide pools: the more I looked, the more I saw. The tiny crustacean and spider mite populations seemed infinite, and there were other things—horsehair worms like coils of copper wire, inch-long fairly shrimps colored iridescent blue and gold. Every imaginable kind of aquatic insect lived in the rivulets—backswimmers, water boatmen, whirligig beetles, water beetles, giant water bugs. In grassy spots, grasshopper-sized eastern chorus frogs inflated orange throat sacs to make calls like thumbnails drawn across the tines of large metal combs. My ears rang for hours after listening to them.

And it wasn't even a real swamp. By late April it had dried up and become an ordinary beech and oak wood. The real central Ohio swamps were even more formidable. Wood frogs, green frogs, spring peepers, green tree frogs, and eastern toads added their voices to the chorus frogs; black-and-yellow-spotted salamanders and blue-mottled Jefferson salamanders crept over the bottom to deposit gelatinous egg masses; six-inch mud turtles sunned on logs, under which, gargoyle-like, lurked two-foot snapping turtles.

The Coyote Hills flatlands didn't measure up to that, although they might have come closer in the past. California flatlands feature perennial vernal pools, where fairy shrimp, newts, and tiger salamanders mingle each winter and spring with chorus frogs, red-legged frogs, and western pond turtles. Giant red copepods that inhabit such pools gather on salamander egg clusters like rose-sized underwater blossoms. The real wildflowers that ring California vernal pools outshine Midwest swamps: masses of blue and gold that change as the pools shrink through the spring. Few remain in the Bay Area, though. I wondered if, left to itself long enough, the soggy expanse I walked through that day would grow vernal pools again within historical time, but since none remained in the vicinity as far as I knew, it seemed unlikely.

I phoned the East Bay Regional Park District to ask about the Coyote Hills flatlands' past and future, but I didn't learn much except that the Alameda County Flood Control Board had jurisdiction over the area and that the permanent marsh would be enlarged as part of a flood control plan. I asked if native vernal pools could be reestablished there, but the planner I talked to didn't seem interested. He said the field where I watched night herons at dusk would be a parking lot and picnic area.

—*Berkeley Monthly*, January 1980

a walk on the ridge lands

It is a steady climb as we walk southward along the ridge. The top narrows as we ascend, and ghost pines and canyon live oaks crowd around the dirt road. Deer hooves and coyote pads mark the soil, still soft from later winter rain. Flickers, jays, and acorn woodpeckers call. The day is overcast, and the ridgetop is in the clouds—we see things fitfully as mist streams past. Sometimes it obscures everything except the road: sometimes it reveals distant ridges. We walk past snow patches from a storm earlier in the month.

Suddenly the clouds open on a coyote on a knoll. It is the same gray as the misty grass, and we see it only because it moves. It is small and short-legged. As it disappears, two taller, rangier coyotes materialize and hurry after it: this is mating season. When they're gone, it is as if they had never been.

We turn eastward and descend the ridge. The slope is dark with bay, live oak, and madrone; loud with running water. It drops steeply to the canyon bottom, where the creek runs high and brown with silt. A few small sycamores grow among tumbled boulders of a rich blue, like lapis lazuli, which contrasts vividly with the cream-and-olive sycamore bark. Upstream, a huge boulder covered with moss and maidenhair fern looms like a ruined castle.

Raccoons have tracked the creek's border. We cross and start up the other slope. It is gentler, rising in a series of terraces covered with valley oak savanna. Some of the oaks are giants, and an isolated madrone could win a prize for the grace and symmetry of its crown. A yellow haze of buttercups sets off the deep green of the grass. The remote place strangely seems more a tended arboretum than a shaggy wilderness, as though esoteric influences keep it weeded and mowed.

We become aware of one less esoteric influence when a red-tailed hawk lands in an oak and eyes a rock outcropping veined with paths connecting burrow entrances. This colony of California ground squirrels must contribute to the tended aspect. The squirrels aren't out today: they don't like wet weather. But the hawk keeps watch as we move on.

Higher up, the savanna terraces run into winding ravines hung with bay and live oak. We pass one of the abandoned homesteads that dot the ridge lands. There are bed frames, chairs, a stove, a sink. There is an enameled water dipper like cowboys drink from in Westerns. But there are no walls, the homestead having burned down, leaving the furnishings open to the sky but, strangely, not vandalized because nobody comes here.

Coulter pines stand at the ravine heads, where frost stays on the grass most of the day. Straighter and bushier than the ghost pines, they give the ridgetop an alpine aspect. Vivacious little streams meander through miniature valleys. As we walk up one, a bobcat bounds away. It is small and slender, with black-banded legs and back. Its white tail patch shows for a moment after the rest of it fades into the pine shadows.

We reach the ridgetop, a narrow plateau covered with open stands of small blue-and-black oak trees growing on gravelly clay worked to a spongy texture by pocket gophers. A lawn of perennial grasses mixed with lupines, poppies, buttercups, larkspurs, and many other wildflowers grows on it, although few are in bloom yet. The oak buds are just beginning to swell and show color. On the ground, fallen black oak leaves—large, yellow, and spiny-lobed—contrast handsomely with pale purple blue oak leaves. If the valley oak savanna is like an arboretum, this is like an orchard.

The first sunshine appears after a day and night of rain. A gulf opens in the mist, and the ridge suddenly overlooks a hundred square miles that show no human presence except a power line and some dirt roads, just peaks, ridges, and canyons—some densely wooded, some grassy, some with olive green dustings of chaparral over red soil.

We head back north, returning in the direction from which we started two nights before. After a few miles, signs of human influence begin to impinge on the strange sense of natural cultivation. There are fewer trees, more annual grasses like wild oats, and the trees show a browse line at three feet from the ground. Soon we see cattle, although these are not the usual polled steers. They are rangy, motley beasts with functional-looking horns. A magpie perches on one's back, while starlings walk among their hooves. They might be in Africa. They don't panic and lumber away: they stand and stare. We give them a wide berth.

We see another bobcat ambling along a lateral ridge a half mile away and watch it for fifteen minutes. It approaches a big oak as though to climb it and then changes its mind. It stands a moment watching something and then lies down and starts to clean itself house cat–style, twitching its tail with pleasure at the emerging sun's warmth. It is much bigger than the bobcat in the pines, and its body is not banded but plain gray, with a golden tinge around the head. It jumps up and stalks something for a moment, then relaxes and sits down, and finally trots of out sight down a gully.

—Berkeley Monthly, 1980

the mountains of running away

the south diablo range

Human dramas often characterize wild places. Everest would be different if famous climbers hadn't died on it. Less operatic dramas characterize less famous places, like the tangle of ridge lands around Mount Hamilton east of San Jose. An encounter that occurred there three months before the U.S. Declaration of Independence was so fleeting that it barely entered history. But it still resonates.

Fray Pedro Font, a Franciscan missionary from Mexico, was the first European to describe the ridge lands, having crossed them with explorer Juan Bautista de Anza's expedition in April 1776. After choosing the site for San Francisco, the expedition tried to reach the gleaming Sierra Nevada via Livermore Valley but found their way blocked by vast marshes in the San Joaquin Valley. Anxious to return to relatively civilized Monterey, Font urged de Anza to take a shortcut across some unknown mountains they saw to the south. De Anza obligingly led them into the range, which they expected to cross in a day. When they camped that night in an arid canyon just a few miles south, Font was having second thoughts.

"In all the journey today we did not see a single Indian," he wrote, "finding only human tracks stamped in the dry mud. It seemed to me that the country is so bad that it could not easily be inhabited by human beings."

Although central California had one of North America's densest native populations, the rugged mountains, now called the Diablo Range after their northernmost extension, Mount Diablo, probably stood empty for most of the year. Bay Area Ohlones and San Joaquin Valley Yokuts mainly passed through seasonally to hunt or to gather acorns, bulbs, and pine nuts.

The Spaniards spent the next day laboriously climbing in and out of canyons, trying to go southwest, but "forced every which way" by the terrain. "All this country which we crossed this day and next is very broken, and the haunt of many bears," Font observed nervously. Finally, they came to some flat land, a "very long valley," where they encountered—briefly—the Diablos' apparently sole human inhabitant. "In the course of the valley," Font wrote, "we saw some ruinous and abandoned little huts, but the only Indian seen was at a distance and running, for as soon as he saw us he fled into the brush of the Sierra like a deer."

The encounter probably occurred in what is now San Antonio Valley, a stretch of oak savanna east of Mount Hamilton. It is unclear why the man was running, whether simply in startled terror at the sudden advent of hairy-faced strangers or from a rumor that they might grab him and herd him into a mission. He had much to fear: the Franciscans who founded nearby Mission Santa Clara meant well, but disease and depression killed most of the people they planned to convert into Christian peasants.

All that was in the future, however. The Spaniards finally straggled back into the known Gilroy Valley two days later, and their fumbling canyon-crawl was such an embarrassment to the highly competent and accomplished de Anza—who earlier had trekked confidently across California's entire desert, from the Colorado River to the coast—that he called the Diablos the Sierra del Chasco, the "Mountains of the Prank."

The "ruinous and abandoned" Ohlone or Yokuts huts are long gone today, of course, and a paved road runs down San Antonio Valley. But it's still easy to visualize that running man, a speck of frantic liberty in a world that Font's magisterial prose was already starting to subdue. Despite the road, the valley is little more inhabited now, and the Diablos remain good mountains to run away into, as I found when I began running away into them in the early 1970s. The very qualities that had repelled Font attracted me—the emptiness and the way the hills led "every which way," twisting around and opening into surprise canyons and sudden vistas. Something about the sky hinted at vast expanses: a feeling of convexity, of opening out.

I found an alluring amalgam of familiarity and exoticism. The oaks, pines, maples, sycamores, and buckeyes had smells and seasonal changes like those of eastern woodlands I grew up with, but the way they grew—scattered in savannas, massed in canyons, gnarled and isolated on ridgetops—had a novel Mediterranean clarity. The savannas seemed African, with their sweeps of grasses and bold wildlife— deer, wild boar, coyotes, eagles, and bobcats. The canyons' aromatic evergreens—bay laurels and madrones—had a subtropical lushness, while the ridgetops, dotted with shaggy Coulter pines and sprinkled with snowfalls, were like glimpses of an ice age.

Novelty seemed inexhaustible in the roughly half million acres—from Livermore to Pacheco Pass—around the Bay Area's highest peaks— 4,209-foot Mount Hamilton, 4,230-foot Mount Isabel, and 4,372-foot Mount Copernicus. And there was good scientific reason for my impression. At the interface of hot Central Valley, humid coast, and cool highlands, the Diablos contain outstanding biodiversity, even for diverse California. I could walk an hour on a dry plateau haunted by whiptail lizards and tarantulas, then suddenly descend into a moist basin with ponds full of frogs, newts, and turtles—it was like stepping from Arizona to Oregon. And that was just the day shift. Nocturnal oddities I might never see lurked in the rocks and ridges—ringtails, spotted skunks, badgers. What I did see after sunset could be startling. Long-eared pallid bats scuttled over the ground hunting crickets and sometimes flew up from under my feet. Once I came on a large toad with a scorpion clamped in its jaws, the stinger curled around one eye.

PREHISTORY

Exploring the Diablos was like entering a remnant of the nine-million-year-old world that fossils have revealed at various East Bay sites, like Blackhawk Ranch. That world, the Miocene epoch, was even more a mixture of the familiar and strange than today's. The coast was a rolling plain with active volcanoes to the east. Rhinos, mastodons, hyena-like dogs, and three-toed horses inhabited it, but so did ground squirrels, rabbits, gray foxes, deer, and pronghorns. Oaks and pines dotted savannas; sycamores and cottonwoods lined streams. California is a very old place.

We don't understand everything about how that coastal plain evolved into today's more rugged landscape, but we have a general idea. Current geological theory suggests that the plain began turning into Font's "bad country" about three million years ago, as two vast tectonic plates that underlie the Pacific Ocean and western North America began to move sideways against each other at an increased rate. The stress fractured coastal bedrock into many active faults, turning the plain into a jumble of ridges and depressions, thrusting up the ridges at a rate of .07 inch a year. Rising peaks created rain shadows, transforming the rolling plain into a mosaic of moist and dry habitats—woodlands on north- and west-facing slopes; chaparral, savanna, and grassland on south- and east-facing ones. Streams lined with gallery forest carved mazes of canyons.

About 1.8 million years ago, the series of climatic fluctuations called the Pleistocene ice age started adding another layer of diversity. Although not high enough for glaciers, Hamilton and other peaks supported a conifer forest like that of the Sierra Nevada today. Relict ponderosa pines still occupy a few high ridges around them. Some wildlife became even stranger than before as lowered sea level allowed eighteen-foot-tall ground sloths and Volkswagen-sized glyptodonts to migrate from South America. Other wildlife became more like today's as elk and grizzlies arrived from Eurasia.

Then, about fifteen thousand years ago, the modern world emerged as the most recent glaciation ended and most large animals vanished. By then the Diablos probably looked very like what Font saw when he called them "very tangled and full of brush, pines, live oaks, oaks, spruce, and other trees."

HARD CLIMBS AND DRY WELLS

The Diablo Range hadn't changed much a century after Font, when the new California State Geological Survey explored it. "Back of the treeless hills that lie along the San Joaquin plain," wrote survey botanist William H. Brewer in his aptly titled memoir, *Up and Down California,* "there rises a labyrinth of ridges, furrowed and separated by deep canyons. . . . It is almost terra incognita. No map represents it, no explorers touch it; a few hunters know something of it, and all unite in giving it a hard name." Exploring "picturesque but desolate" canyons south from today's Corral Hollow, Brewer and his men encountered pronghorn herds, cottonwood groves full of "squawking and screaming" blue herons, and ridgetops that had been completely "dug over by bears for roots."

When Brewer and his crew climbed Mount Hamilton in June 1861, it was the first recorded ascent. Although farms already "enclosed" the Santa Clara Valley below, the mountain remained so trackless that the geologists underestimated the distance to the summit by six miles. "We had attained an altitude of nearly three thousand feet, when we came upon another deep and steep canyon, cutting us off from the peak," Brewer wrote. "Here we left our mules and proceeded on foot about three miles and reached the peak about 4 p.m." The surveyors noted, a bit peevishly, that Laurentine Hamilton, a local Presbyterian minister who accompanied them, reached the summit first because he wasn't carrying instruments. They named the peak after first-up Reverend Hamilton, but only after the survey's leader, Josiah Whitney, had declined the honor.

Civilization did change the Diablos in the next century. Homesteaders moved in, extirpating elk, grizzlies, and pronghorns; building roads, cabins, and many miles of fences. George Thomas Jr., a Morgan Hill attorney whose family has ranched locally since 1877, told me that seven or eight homesteads, as well as a school with thirty-five students, once occupied the two thousand acres his family now owns. There was so much social activity that people came from San Jose to attend dances. Little trace of that time remains. Water was too scarce for small family farms, and most homesteaders sold out and left in the 1920s and '30s.

Civilization's best-known mark on the Diablo Range is idiosyncratic. In the 1870s, an aging San Francisco bachelor named James Lick felt an urge to commemorate his life, and when friends suggested he endow an astronomical observatory, he liked the idea. A former piano maker who prospered in gold rush real estate, Lick spent much of his fortune to have a thirty-six-inch refracting telescope installed in a hardwood-paneled dome on 160 acres atop Mount Hamilton. He died in 1876, before he could see the result of his largesse, but when his friends donated the observatory to the University of California in 1888, he was present nonetheless. They'd installed him in a tomb under the telescope, where he remains.

BUTTERFLIES AND MONSTER HOMES

It might almost have been 1861 when I started running away into the Diablos in the early 1970s, because like Brewer and his crew I could hike for days and not see anybody. A few abandoned homesteads stood undisturbed, their domestic contents intact. The solitude was unusual even then, when much land along I-80 between Oakland and San Jose was still open fields inhabited by pheasants and burrowing owls.

Suburban growth has since become more obtrusive. Corporations and speculators acquired most of the former homesteads, and although they managed them as ranches or hunting clubs, it was with an idea to future expansion. In the 1970s, the development firm Kaiser-Aetna planned a large subdivision on the Dowdy Ranch north of Highway 152, the lonesome road that crosses the Diablos at Pacheco Pass. Investors at the Lakeview Meadows Ranch near Anderson Reservoir east of U.S. 101 hoped to build a hundred-thousand-resident "new town" to be planned by Castle and Cooke, developers of Sea Ranch on the Sonoma coast.

Running away had its supporters too, however. In 1972 Josephine Grant willed her father's 9,250-acre ranch west of Mount Hamilton to charities, which then sold it to Santa Clara County as the Joseph D. Grant Regional Park. In 1953 Sada S. Coe gave Santa Clara County a 12,500-acre ranch that her father and uncle had worked at Pine Ridge, south of Mount Hamilton, and in 1958 that became the nucleus of Henry W. Coe State Park. Henry Coe has since grown to more than eighty-one thousand acres, including a twenty-two-thousand-acre Wilderness Area, and is now northern California's largest state park. In 1974 I could walk around most of the park in a day. In April 2000, a day hike didn't get me halfway across.

A lesson of the past two decades, unfortunately, has been that big subdivisions can impact even big parks. Urban growth seemed inexorable in the late-twentieth-century boom years, and in 2000 I got a strong taste of this south of San Jose, where a Stanford biologist named Stewart Weiss was studying an endangered butterfly, the bay checkerspot. The species mainly survives on a serpentine ridge that rises out of the Santa Clara Valley just east of U.S. 101, across from the Riverside Golf Course. Soils weathered from calcium-poor serpentine bedrock are infertile to invasive exotic weeds, so native plants persist in unusual numbers. The bay checkerspot depends on the natives for food, and Weiss's study area may be the only place with enough of them to permanently support a viable butterfly population.

I'd driven past the ridge many times on U.S. 101, and it had seemed just another expanse of grazing land. When Weiss showed me around in April, it was one of the most spectacular native wildflower displays I've seen, acres of yellow goldfields, tidy tips, and cream cups interspersed with pink wild onion, owl clover, and linanthus. Those were just the common species. Weiss said he'd counted more than two hundred native ones in all, some of which grow nowhere else. Even big thistles in streambeds—which I'd thought were just weedy milk thistles—were rare natives.

It was an extraordinarily vibrant place—the flowers thronged with butterflies and bees, the small creeks full of tadpoles—but a beleaguered one. Weiss pointed out a patchwork of pending subdivisions and industrial parks in the valley below. Nearer, to the north, the "monster homes" of the new Silver Creek subdivision climbed the hillsides. Even the spring air flowing from the advancing suburbs threatened the wildflowers. "This place is a funnel for smog," Weiss said. His studies had shown that polluted air could deposit nitrogen oxide on the ridge's soil in large amounts, as much as ten pounds per acre every year. Nitrogen is a nutrient, so this fallout can significantly increase serpentine soil's fertility, allowing exotic grasses to crowd out natives.

The serpentine ridge was a first line of defense for the Diablos, and Weiss was trying to get it preserved. This would make sense even without threatened flora and fauna, because landslide-prone serpentine is bad for building. A conservation trust agreement with a landfill company on the ridge's Kirby Canyon area had provided protection for the past decade. It wasn't permanent, however, and protecting any land beside a major freeway is tricky. The ridge was outside San Jose's "greenline" urban growth boundary, so city services weren't supposed to go there, but subdividers had mounted legal and political challenges. "There's a ridiculously small amount of habitat here with long-term protection," Weiss concluded.

Yet sprawl may have met something like its match in the Diablos. The Nature Conservancy is one of the more powerful conservation organizations, with more than a million members and well-tuned financial machinery for snatching land from subdividing jaws. In 1997, when the organization applied a new "biological scoping" process to the central California coast region, the Diablo Range came up as a "portfolio site," large enough to "define and contain" the region's diversity. So the Conservancy initiated a Mount Hamilton Project, with the goal of protecting four hundred thousand acres within seven years. A map of its acquisition priorities resembled a pair of angelic wings outspread to the east and west of Henry Coe, a configuration that would block subdivisions from cozying up to the park boundaries. Attorney George Thomas Jr., who wanted to maintain his family's century-old ranch as such, called the project a "dream come true."

Project director Mike Sweeney, a former aide to Interior Secretary Bruce Babbitt, talked about the dream on a May 2000 visit to O'Connell Ranch, a new Conservancy acquisition north of Anderson Reservoir. "The 1990s were among the longest sustained urban expansions in our history," he said. "Small preserves weren't protecting biodiversity enough, so in the last five years we've been launching big ones. When the project started, this was an area where the subdivision wave hadn't crested yet. A relatively small number of large ranches existed, and land prices weren't out of sight. We can move faster than government agencies to acquire land in a market like that." He pointed at a ridge to the southeast, where the Conservancy had acquired the Lakeview Meadows Ranch from developers in 1999. "Lakeview Meadows is an example," he said. "They were trying to put monster homes in view of Henry Coe headquarters, but it was a little early for that, and they saw a chance to cash out with us quickly."

The Mount Hamilton Project planned to place some of its acquisitions in public ownership through sale to Santa Clara County and the California Department of Parks. Even the Conservancy couldn't afford to preserve the whole range, however, so it planned to sell other properties back into private hands, retaining development rights and working with ranchers to improve range management and protect riparian areas.

"The way we design a big project like this is not to say you can't develop here," Sweeney said. "We try to control development so it won't impair the ecosystem's ability to function. The main problems we're trying to control in the Mount Hamilton area are residential sprawl, overgrazing, and exotic species invasion."

Walking around the O'Connell Ranch, we saw examples of all three problems. Leapfrog subdivisions sprawled around Anderson Reservoir to the southeast, and exotic weeds from two centuries of heavy grazing covered the hillsides. It was still a beautiful place, dotted with oaks, bays, and buckeyes and teeming with songbirds and butterflies. "A problem with these inland areas has been that they're relatively unknown, so you don't get as much public support to save things as you do on the coast," Sweeney said. "What we're doing with an acquisition like this is trying to improve opportunities for people to get out and see what's here while preserving habitat for species of special concern, like tiger salamanders, Pacific pond turtles, and red-legged frogs.

The project moved fast. In late 2000, the state bought the 4,413-acre Stevenson Ranch, which the Conservancy had acquired in July. Once zoned for at least forty "executive mansions," the ranch was added to Henry Coe State Park. Two huge properties east of the park (Simon Newman and Romero), acquired by the Conservancy in 1998, were resold to ranchers minus the development rights, which were transferred to public agencies. "There are beautiful old sycamores out there," Sweeney said of the big ranches, "but no young ones. They kept getting cropped, along with all kinds of other species. You can't blame the ranchers: fences are expensive, and the cattle need water. Our role is to allow them to continue without devastating the area. And just in the last few years, we're starting to see rapid recovery in places that have been eaten back for a century."

If the Mount Hamilton Project meets its goals, it will help keep the Diablos like they were when Font and Brewer explored them. This should help protect extant biodiversity, like the outstanding mountain lion and golden eagle populations, and also allow for reintroduction of some extirpated species. The Department of Fish and Game has reintroduced tule elk and pronghorns, although hikers seldom see them because they live mostly in privately owned valleys. California condors from the population reintroduced at the Pinnacles probably will venture farther north. Grizzly bears won't be back anytime soon, although wild boars, which have replaced them in their omnivorous, rooting ecological niche, are an impressive presence. I once watched a very large one that I had surprised in pond wallow run up a nearly vertical slope without the least sign of effort. Black bears are also expanding their range into former grizzly country.

Like the grizzly, one thing that is unlikely to return to the Diablos soon is the solitude that prevailed in Font and Brewer's times, or even in the 1970s. I passed dozens of hikers on my April 2000 visit to Henry Coe, and that was on a weekday. When park ranger Doug Meyers took me around the backcountry in May, he expressed amazement at how much the park had changed in the time he'd worked there. "When I first came, in 1978, there might have been ten trail signs in the park," he said. "Now there are probably about two thousand signs and over two hundred miles of trail. I don't even think we've begun to see the increased visitation that's going to result from the changes that have taken place in the Bay Area in the past five years. It'll be in the coming years that we get the full impact."

Yet the Diablos' sense of inexhaustible remoteness and diversity remains. It took us all morning to traverse the park from south to north in Meyers's four-wheel-drive patrol vehicle. The temperature that day reached 102 degrees. Besides us, a coyote and a tom turkey were the only sizable vertebrates that had ventured out in it. The heat felt like a wall by noon, when we reached the park's northeastern boundary, where a cliff called the Rooster Comb looms above Orestimba Creek, a tributary of the San Joaquin. The creek had already sunk underground except for a few puddles, but they teemed with insect and amphibian larvae, all rushing to complete their life cycles before summer's *real* heat clamped down. Little blue oaks and ghost pines dotted the hills in every direction. It seemed about as wild a place as there can be in twenty-first-century California.

The Diablos still have their secrets. When I was on Mount Hamilton's summit in April 2000, I idly wondered if they had built the observatory on some unique plant species. A few months later, I met a botanist at UC–Berkeley's Jepson Herbarium, Barbara Erter, who recently had helped to name an endemic carrot family wildflower, *Lomatium observatorium*, found by an observant photographer on the summit in 1996. A place where dozens of people have been walking every day for over a century had yielded a new species. And there probably are still places in the Diablos—arroyos, chaparral thickets, cliff overhangs—where no humans have ever walked at all.

—*Bay Nature*, April–June 2001

AUTHOR'S NOTE: *The future of Hamilton's summit clouded in 2014 when the university decided to cut funding for the Lick Observatory and move its astronomy research to telescopes in Hawaii. After protests from students and faculty, the university restored funding, but it's unclear what will become of the observatory and its ancient occupant. Given urbanization, the stars above Hamilton must be much less visible than they were when Brewer climbed it, although declining research finances were the main reason given for the move.*

cultures and creatures

starlings

It is November in northern Europe seven thousand years ago. Heather and birches grow on hills, willows and sphagnum moss in bogs: they form a thin plant layer over the stones and clay left by a retreating ice sheet. No songbirds call in the frosty birches as the sky reddens at dawn, but a noise begins to come from the bogs. It is not the miscellany of songbird territorial calls: there is something monolithic about it, and it rises to a roar as thousands of blackish, short-tailed birds pour out of the willows like a hail of darts.

The darts coalesce as they rise and form a sphere, then an oval. A starling flock is coming out to fly up the valley, and little in nature matches the amorphous elegance of it. Other birds display more color or grace in flocking, but starlings are unexcelled in coordinated movement. Although individual starlings or groups leave or join the flock, it remains a single entity, flickering as the birds bank or swerve in unison, a living smudge against the skyline, sometimes dark, sometimes nearly transparent, pulsating like a huge, weightless amoeba.

A herd of aurochs grazes on the plain above the valley, wild cattle the size of small elephants. As the flock nears them, it circles, lights briefly in a birch grove, then flattens into a kind of dense mist as the starlings alight on the herd. Some run among the aurochs' hooves, picking through manure for seeds or parasite larvae: some land on the broad backs and comb the hair for sheltering insects. After feeding, most of the flock disperses to rest or forage for wild fruit and seeds, but they stay near the herd and come back to feed again when the sun is low.

At dusk, the hail of darts funnels back into the bog willows, and before long not a bird is visible, although the noise continues awhile. When the stars emerge, incredibly brilliant by today's standards, the roost is silent.

Light snow falls during the night, and some of the birds move south the next day. Starlings from farther north take their place, and it is not until the solstice, when snow lies deep and aurochs and other ungulates have retreated south into forests, that the roost is completely abandoned. The flocks pass on to southern European marshes or across a widening Mediterranean to the savannas of what is now the Sahara. Others converge on Middle Eastern marshes and grasslands, where some get their first taste of orchards and vineyards.

Starlings belong to a large avian family, the Sturnidae, most of which are showy birds of Africa and tropical Asia. The talking mynah is one; starlings are mimics too. How *Sturnus vulgaris*, the common starling, adapted to life in the north isn't clear, but it did so very successfully, although the species's mass flocking depended, as in Africa, on large ungulate herds living in fairly open areas. As forest covered warming Europe in the postglacial period, starlings may have undergone a population slump. But help was on the way, as growing human populations cut forest and ran large cattle herds on the resultant fields and pastures. Starlings nest in tree holes, but buildings make acceptable substitutes.

Then things got even better for northern starlings. In an unprecedented burst of goodwill, nineteenth-century humans took the species to the New World. Legend has it that the first North American ones nested in the eaves of New York's American Museum of Natural History in 1891. An ornithologist and Shakespeare enthusiast named Scheifflin is said to have introduced them in an attempt to bring all the birds mentioned by the bard here. If so, he failed, since only starlings caught on. (English sparrows and rock doves had arrived earlier.) But starlings caught on in a big way. Although it was too late for the bison herds they might have exploited a few years before, they found plenty of cattle herds. They colonized the continent from Alaska to Mexico in less than seventy years.

Starlings also developed an ability to thrive in industrial landscapes, both urban and rural. Habitat destruction and pollution are no problem to birds that can nest in factories and forage in landfills. Agribusiness, with its giant monocultures, does not discourage starlings if a roost exists within twenty miles. And starlings make their own contributions to habitat destruction and pollution, preempting native birds' nest holes, contaminating livestock feed, and depositing guano a foot deep under roosts. One roost in Virginia's Dismal Swamp accommodated an estimated twenty million birds.

The dawn sky above College Avenue in Oakland is gray with fog, but linnets, robins, and titmice have been singing for a half hour. A starling emerges from the eaves of a house, perches on the roof rain gutter, and joins the chorus with a series of low whistles, not very musical but enough to call her mate. As still-migrating cedar waxwings flock around a holly bush, the starlings fly into an ornamental birch, where they pick at catkins, moving around the trunk in spirals like woodpeckers, then descend to the ground to look for insects.

Their yellow beaks show clearly against the dark earth as they probe among bark chips. A month before, in February, the beaks were gray. They turned yellow as the birds' gonads swelled in response to the lengthening days, releasing a color-changing hormone. Their plumage is glossier than it was in the winter: the ocher specks that tipped the feathers of their fall molt have worn off, leaving the showy iridescent parts. Swelling gonads also caused emotional changes that led the birds to leave the flock and settle in the eaves, although they're not alone. Another starling pair occupies another corner of the house. Starlings tolerate high nesting density in favorable sites, which gives them an advantage in maintaining population and in increasing it when conditions are good.

One of the starlings under the birch picks up a bit of straw, then drops it absentmindedly. A car door slams, and the pair flies to a TV aerial. From there they see the other pair bathing in the rain gutter, so they join them with great splashing. Then they all dart off in different directions. One flies back to the eave, hones her beak, and looks around cautiously, then disappears under it. In a while, her mate flies up with a twig, but the house door opens and he ducks into the gutter. Nesting starlings are seldom seen during the human workday. This unassuming family life is another source of population maintenance. They'd be more vulnerable if they nested in noisy groups.

A few weeks later, the pair is nest building seriously. Starling nests are untidy heaps of straw and twigs, on which they lay, in April, five to seven green eggs. Nestlings hatch and fledge by June, although unmated males sometimes sneak in and destroy nests. If all goes well, the parents then raise another brood, which can mean there will be five or seven times as many starlings in an area after the breeding season as before. The birds then leave nesting areas, which can be in wilderness as well as cities, and join flocks for their customary mass feedings and migrations. But life gets harder for them then.

For a little while, the pale green glow of the cities to the west and the yellow glare of the power plant and gypsum mill across the Sacramento River obscure the November dawn. Then it begins to spread across the sky, and hills appear on the horizon. Pheasants squawk metallically in the harvested fields behind the river levees, and geese formations straggle overhead like sooty cobwebs. As the sun rises, red and huge in the smog of freeway exhaust and burning rice fields, an island grown with willow thickets and tule marshes emits a wave of noise as thousands of red-winged blackbirds, Brewer's blackbirds, and starlings emerge to fly over the levees and light on fields or power lines. The blackbirds form scattered, straggling flocks; the starlings larger, denser ones. The flocks billow and swarm across the flats, then move toward the hills.

The sun is yellow and bright when they reach the feedlot, which looks strange among the bare brown hills—acres of brightly painted mixing and storage bins and pens full of steers. The blackbirds scatter to feed on waste grain, but the starlings are more discriminating. Ignoring unused pens, they concentrate on the feeding troughs and manure of the full ones, eating the expensive fare that cattle being fattened are given. That day, the ground of the pens is also sprinkled with blue-dyed chicken feed pellets that have been treated with a compound called Trichloro-p-toluidine-hydrochloride. Many starlings eat varying quantities of these.

The flock fans out into the hills after feeding as usual, but then something unusual begins to happen. By late afternoon, starlings that have eaten a lot of pellets crouch on the ground or fences with feathers fluffed as though they're cold, although the California sun is warm enough. Their blood is running sluggishly as it fills with uric acid from disabled kidneys. These birds have trouble breathing, then lose consciousness and die without cries or convulsions that might disturb other birds. So the flock feeds at the lot again before it returns to the river roost.

During the night, birds that have eaten small or moderate amounts of the blue pellets also die. The next morning, after unaffected birds have flown, several thousand dead starlings litter the marsh, along with a few hundred blackbirds and two crows. Some corpses still cling to their roosts, and a Cooper's hawk glides in to grab one of these. Since the dead starling has metabolized and excreted most of the slow-acting poison, the hawk shows no noticeable ill effects from eating it. Within two weeks, birds migrating from the north have replaced most of the dead birds in the roost.

—Clear Creek, 1972

the fifth season

This August I moved back to the Bay Area after living in Ohio for several years. I'd grown used to the intense green of summers, and I looked at the brown grass here with something of Midwest disapproval. At the same time, I was glad to see the yellow hills. During the five years I'd lived here, I'd grown to like the spiky desiccation of California's dry time. It gave bite to an environment that otherwise might have been tediously benign.

The old complaint about California not having seasons is wrong. In fact, it has more than the Midwest. The period from mid-July through September is a fifth season, a second plant dormancy. Fall's bright, crisp days go from October to mid-November; winter's storms and occasional frosts to mid-February; spring's manic flowering to mid-May; and summer's lingering greenery to July, at least in wet years. The fifth season after that should have a name, but I can't think of one, and our culture doesn't want to acknowledge it anyway. Millions throng the Sierra to romp in December snow, but few want to romp in blazing Bay Area August's dry grass, although that would be more appropriate to human evolution. An African savanna hominid would be happier in a Bay Area August than in a Sierra January.

For all its harshness, however, the fifth season is fragile. It quickly shows the marks of abuse. Native perennial grasses and forbs are beautiful and well adapted to the dry season, but agribusiness and competition from introduced annual grasses have pushed them aside. A golden August swath of bunchgrass and yellow or white tarweeds turns into a dusty scar with overgrazing or trampling, impacts that harm reproduction of native oak woodland and savanna as well.

Partly because it is so easy to degrade, we treat the fifth season as a lapse of taste—we cover it with evergreens and lawns. For every native plant garden, there are thousands of exotic plant ones ranging from banana and bougainvillea to birch and barberry. Freeway borders feature oleander, eucalyptus, pyracantha—even some out-of-place redwoods struggling against ozone and sunburn—anything to avoid showing a bare branch or a patch of dry grass. But the herbicide-bared dirt and litter under the straggling greenery give the lie to it.

We should come to terms with the fifth season and give it a place alongside the traditional four, but there are problems. Wildfire is the big one. California plants and animals are adapted to periodic fires—California suburbs aren't. It's nice to have a house nestled in greenery until what Raymond Chandler called "the red wind" from the deserts blows for a few days. Then—as crisp leaves spiral in little tornadoes across driveways—homeowners may wish for a yard of bare dirt, like Spanish California's adobes.

Wildfire is a reason why freeway borders aren't kept in grass here as they are in the Midwest. Grassed California highway borders mostly would be brown and dead from June to November, highly flammable, and smoke doesn't harmonize with aggressive driving habits. Freeway grass in Ohio is dead and brown from October to March, but there's little fire danger then, and in spring it quickly comes alive with grasses and wildflowers that change through the summer and fall: in April dandelions and clover; in May, daisies and birdsfoot trefoil; in June, thistles, fleabane, and hawkweed; in July, milkweed and black-eyed Susan; in August, sunflowers and ironweed; in September, asters and goldenrod.

Wildfire aside, if the Department of Transportation lost its oleanders and let the grasses and forbs grow, California's roadsides could be a lot less ugly. They mostly would be exotic weeds at first. But the Ohio highway border plants are largely exotic weeds too, and many natives grow mixed in. Horticulture crews freed from maintaining evergreens might restore some native grasses and wildflowers. Fire management of railroad rights-of-way preserved Midwest prairie plants that farming otherwise threatened. Railroad rights-of-way may have a comeback someday: we can't afford freeways forever.

Civilization has always had a tricky relationship with "Mediterranean" climates like California's. With their gentle fertility, they can seem limitless, but fragile dry seasons offer large arenas for destructiveness and carelessness. Newspapers talk about "the dark side of the California dream," but sunlight provokes more violence than moonlight. Early California murder trials recognized the "red winds" as extenuating circumstances.

Despite the problems, I think we lose an important element of change by covering up and neglecting the fifth season. Change is life's universal attribute, and it is often scary, but it can't be stopped. California cities begin to look embalmed with their eternal greenery after the novelty wears off. Like most easterners (I grew up in New England), I liked eternal springtime when I first came to California, but I've come to suspect it. The old California's wrinkled body may be unflattering, but it is the true matrix of renewal here.

—*Berkeley Monthly*, January 1979

gardening

I got interested in gardening when I was driving a Yellow Cab on the night shift in San Francisco. Such an urban occupation seems incongruous with a bucolic one, but that was the attraction. My first fare was a bandaged cabbie just released from the emergency room after running through a plate-glass window to escape an armed mugger. That was in the early 1970s, when the Zodiak's serial murder victims included cabbies. It suddenly seemed wonderful—visionary—that I might get at least part of a living from growing things, from natural harmony, and that I could enlist the support of other living things like earthworms, soil bacteria, and insect-eating songbirds in doing so.

When I moved out of the city not too long afterward, I started a garden by digging up some ground, churning manure into it, and throwing seeds in. I didn't get much of a crop, but since I hadn't invested much, I found the tsunami of weeds that broke over my backyard plot interesting. The weeds usurped my patch of cultivation in so many ways, and there were so many kinds—bindweed, curly dock, mallow, mustard, sow thistle. I hadn't known weeds were so resourceful.

My gardening skills were slow to improve. I'd go out with a spading fork on a spring day and fling lettuce, radish, and pea seeds into soil that was dark and moist after its winter sleep. I'd fuss over the seedlings for a few weeks, but as summer advanced and the soil got paler and thirstier, I'd get distracted. I wouldn't get much more than a meal's worth before the pea vines withered and the radishes and lettuces flowered. I probably wouldn't have gotten past that stage if I hadn't married someone with a more practical attitude. My wife worked the soil enough that the plants got their roots into it, and she fertilized and watered it enough that they could get something out of it, and we started to get significant produce. This didn't motivate me to be much more painstaking, but it did provide me with a substantial garden to contemplate. That modified my original vision of gardens as sites of natural harmony.

Gardening is participation in the natural world, all right, but it is about as harmonious as a night in North Beach during my Yellow Cab career, when hordes of tourists, prostitutes, sailors, dope dealers, and narcs surged in and out of my taxi as I careened over the steep cobbled streets and cable car tracks. Vegetables are like cab passengers in that one never knows what they will do, or if they will pay. Weeds are dependable: they are certain to grow on any patch of disturbed ground, and to flower and bear fruit. Vegetables aren't, but they are sure to disturb their benefactor's peace of mind in various ways, even if they do bear fruit.

From an evolutionary viewpoint, a garden is the essence of disturbance, a ramshackle pseudo-ecosystem originated piecemeal from seeds and tubers on prehistoric middens. Most garden plants not only thrive on, but demand, constant disturbance. We call that cultivation, but anyone who has dug into the dirt and turned up a clod of hysterical earthworms can see what is happening to their little world. From a worm's-eye view, a garden is place of dizzying cataclysm, as mountains of compost and manure land on the soil to be devoured by the overgrown mutants we call garden flowers and vegetables.

My garden vision had included the idea that I could build a fertile soil; that some point would arise wherein the soil was finished and I could stop shoveling manure and compost. But a garden's appetite for such fodder is as endless as any organism's. My double-dug raised beds shrank inexorably through the long, dry summers, and by the end they were just as powdery and pebbly as when I first dug them. Gardens aren't really conducive to progressive notions. They don't so much accumulate virtues as consume them.

This isn't to say that I had to start from scratch each year. My wife created many nice beds of perennial flowers and herbs, although even she wasn't confident about them. She marched the plants around from bed to bed, as though to keep them fit. If a bed was particularly flourishing, that meant something would have to be done about it. And of course the perennials devoured compost and manure just as relentlessly as the annuals.

Flowers and vegetables also confounded expectation by replanting themselves. Melons appeared in the bean beds; tomatoes in the lettuce and spinach; giant, orange cucumbers in the squash. Huge borage and potato plants shot up in paths. Things like calendula, catnip, chamomile, and dill grew everywhere. Despite my vision of natural harmony, this vegetable generosity didn't please me. It seemed too extraneous and untidy, which exposed a self-serving side to my vision. I wanted natural harmony on my terms.

If my gardening vision was a disappointment, it was an interestingly surprising one, although by no means all the surprises were pleasant. I was forking a bed one day when a reddish furred creature suddenly appeared at my feet, baring its teeth. It was a pocket gopher, and it had reason for distress: I'd accidentally skewered it in its burrow. I ended its suffering with a rock and felt a disquieting mix of satisfaction and sadness. None of the gardeners I told about it felt the slightest sympathy for the gopher, rather envy at my luck in disposing of it so easily. Still, it had reminded me of interesting times in wild places, watching gophers push earth out of their burrows, or watching coyotes and weasels hunting them.

The encounter brought up an aspect of gardening not much mentioned in books about its merits. The backyard plots that promise to be gardens are occupied already, not as spectacularly as wilder places, but just as fully, and cultivation must sweep a lot of that aside. Of course, no organism lives without sweeping others aside. Still, there are options about how much to sweep aside, especially if one doesn't depend on the garden for a livelihood or even for significant economy.

On the whole, I've found more interest in garden inhabitants than I have in vegetables. The pocket gopher, for example, is a marvelous creature that people might pay to see if it were rare and exotic instead of an ineradicable component of soil ecology in North America's drier regions. Indeed, gophers have made the soil there to a considerable degree. Every year, they cover much of the West with soil pushed out of their burrows, otherwise sterile, compacted dirt they have broken up, aerated, and fertilized with their droppings.

No creature is better evolved to cultivate dry soil than the pocket gopher. It is built like a bulldozer, with powerfully enlarged shoulders and forepaws for pushing dirt and reduced hindquarters for life in tight surroundings. Its head is even more ingenious, especially the mouth. Its incisors are never dull because they grow continually, and its lips close completely behind them so it can cut roots or break ground without eating dirt. Fur-lined pouches outside its cheeks (the "pockets" of its name) allow it to carry food or nesting material while it burrows with teeth and forepaws. Even gopher reproduction is adapted to tunneling. The female's pelvis is too narrow to give birth, so when she becomes pregnant, ovarian hormones dissolve her pubic bones. She spends the rest of her life without them.

Gophers used their equipment to make tunnel systems so vast that startled Great Plains explorers found themselves sinking into dry ground as though it were quicksand. French trappers called such places *gaufres*, "honeycombs," Anglicized as "gopher." One individual's tunnel system can cover an acre, with a five-hundred-foot main tunnel and many smaller ones leading to nests, larders, and privies. Soil mounds pushed from tunnels can be a foot high and ten feet across, although they're usually smaller. In some places, strange hillocky prairies may be relics of exceptionally large or industrious prehistoric gophers.

Of course, such feats are less entertaining when performed in one's garden than in the wild. Gopher damage can seem wanton, since they sometimes destroy plants inadvertently while burrowing. Rows of tomatoes and peppers reduced to wilted hulks during tunnel construction have driven me to a cold sweat. And of course they eat vegetables too, especially those in the bean family. A gopher had a burrow entrance at every patch of beans in one garden of mine—once vigorous plants that it worried to dejected remnants over the course of a summer. It toppled some plants and dragged them whole into its burrow. I couldn't help feeling that it might just have picked some beans and left the plants.

Fortunately for gardeners, gophers are not colonial like their relatives, the ground squirrels and prairie dogs. Although burrow systems may get entangled, giving the impression of a colony, each gopher keeps to its own, sealing it off and defending it against intruders. So having an established resident gopher has its merits, since much of the damage they do occurs during tunnel construction. After I had accidentally skewered the gopher, damage increased markedly as another moved in and started digging its burrow. Then it decreased again after construction finished. Except for some egregious insults to flowers and lettuces, there was surprisingly little damage after that. Gophers are supposed to like the onion family, but a row of leeks went untouched.

The other garden mammals common here, moles, are also solitary, and are less of a challenge to gardeners since they eat animals instead of plants. Indeed, they eat many plant-damaging animals like cutworms as well as beneficial ones like earthworms. They dislike disturbed soil and do most of their burrowing in lawns—one reason for not having a lawn in this climate. When I had a small lawn beside one garden, the moles and gophers never crossed between them. Moles often tunnel just below the surface, leaving a visible ridge, and they push dirt out of their burrows in conical mounds instead of gophers' delta-shaped ones.

Gopher and mole burrows shelter many other inhabitants, most of them garden-friendly insect eaters. Some of the biggest, fattest toads I've seen inhabited garden gopher holes. One would emerge as I was watering a bean patch every day at sunset: I'm not sure if it liked the shower or if the water flowing into its hideout disturbed it. The muffled creaking calls of little toad relatives, western chorus frogs, also came from the holes. Less noticeable residents may include salamanders, lizards, and snakes—from little sharp-tailed snakes to king snakes and the eponymous gopher snakes. Other interesting creatures I've found in gardens probably benefit from gopher burrows. Sun spiders are cricket-like arachnids that live mainly in deserts, but they appear here in hot, dry weather. The purplish local scorpion species can sting, but not dangerously. Jerusalem crickets remind me of little men in Japanese lacquered armor. Velvet ants are wingless wasps that appear to be wearing peroxide wigs. Little tan praying mantises probably don't live in burrows, but they seem part of this menagerie. I've never found a tarantula or a rattlesnake in a garden, probably because I've never had one in a previously unoccupied property.

I've put kidnapped gopher snakes down garden gopher holes once or twice, but it's a pointless exercise, since the snake will leave after it eats the gopher, and then another gopher will move in. The problem with such "biological control" is that predators need a constant supply of prey, which the backyard garden often can't produce. And if it can, that usually means there are too many vegetable eaters for the predators to control entirely. Songbirds that spend every hour of the day relaying bugs to nestlings don't make a dent in the bug supply, and a lot of the animals they consume are neutral or beneficial anyway. A pair of robins at one garden seemed to feed mostly bug-eating centipedes to their young.

Invertebrate damage to gardens is less conspicuous than gopher damage, but of course much more important. Many attack plants at the seedling stage, which is frustrating because it is so inconspicuous. One day, the seedlings are there; the next, they're not. I got an insight into seedling-eater numbers once when I dug up a manure pile that had lain undisturbed for some time. I involuntarily jumped back in surprise as I pulled up the first clod. I don't think I've ever seen a greater density of animal life. Representatives of most major invertebrate orders thronged the interface of wild oat roots and aged manure like diplomats at an OPEC meeting.

The most numerous ones were colored a dull gray appropriate for diplomats—oval, many-segmented wood lice, land relatives of shrimp and crabs. They covered every square inch—all ages, from violet-gray youngsters the size of apple seeds to pumpkin-seed-sized adults. Almost as numerous were reddish-brown earwigs, slender insects with pincer-like cerci on their back ends, which they raised threateningly at me. They are named for the belief that they crawl into ears, which may happen accidentally, although they are more given to destroying vegetable seedlings, as are the slugs and snails I also found in abundance.

The crustaceans, insects, and mollusks comprised the manure's grazing herds. The predators were scarcer but more diverse. Wiry purple-violet centipedes snaked amid the gray wood lice like flames licking at charcoal briquettes, although their color soon faded to duller reddish brown in the sunlight. Grayish spiders with jaws adapted to cracking wood louse carapaces stood among the swarming crustaceans like wolves in a bison herd. A stout red-and-black jumping spider goggled big-eyed at the commotion I'd stirred up, but a long-legged orb weaver spider sat aloof in her web among the oat stems. Another arachnid, a gray-and-white wolf spider, seemed overwhelmed by my presence, until I looked closely and saw that a swarm of baby spiders on her abdomen hindered her movements. Four yellow-and-brown Jerusalem crickets towered ponderously above the horde, although they belied the elephantine impression by quickly digging themselves into the soil.

Plants that get beyond the seedling stage are easier to defend. Tobacco hornworms that infest tomato plants reach sausage size, although their leaf-patterned green color camouflages the caterpillars as they chew languorously on tomatoes. But their dark green feces on leaves are a giveaway, and once found they are easily picked off. Hornworms are named for the wicked-looking spikes on their tails. When molested, they rear back, make gnashing sounds, and wriggle as though ready to sink the "horn" into one's hand, although I never tested that. They are the larvae of the Carolina sphinx moth, a handsome species with an orange-banded abdomen and intricately patterned wings that comes out in the evening to sip nectar from flowers like a crepuscular hummingbird. I didn't mind losing some tomatoes to have sphinx moths in the flower beds.

I've lost more tomatoes to frost than hornworms, and such physical factors are more of an obstacle to gardens than biotic ones. It often seemed as though tomatoes were just ripening when cold September nights kept them green on the vine. And backyard soils can be inhospitable, refusing to produce plants even when unmolested by pests. Gophers and insects alike spared some okra I planted, but the plants never grew more than six inches anyway. The dozen or so pods they produced were bigger than they were. Weeds can be an advantage in such situations, since they respond to watering more vigorously, loosening the soil and pumping nutrients to the surface.

Gardens have mysteries as well as surprises. The speed with which the seedling-eater horde in that old manure pile disappeared into the ground as I dug it up was as startling as its abundance. The same thing happened each time I pulled up a clod: a mob scene, then an empty stage aside from a few loitering spiders. Even the snails and slugs made themselves scarce somehow. When I transferred the last clod to a wheelbarrow, no sign of life remained on the dry, hard-packed clay under it.

Toads that inhabited derelict backyards where I've gardened appeared and vanished just as mysteriously. Once when I emptied a bucket of stony soil I'd dug up, one of the "stones" squeaked indignantly, then waddled off and inserted itself into an inch-long crevice in a pile of boards, an impressive feat since the toad itself was six inches wide. It just flattened out and flowed between the boards. I feared my removal of debris under which I originally found them would discourage the toads, so I built them some little dugouts in compensation, but I never found a toad in one. I wondered whether they had moved away to less disturbed places or had stayed on and adjusted their behavior so I wouldn't disturb them.

Some mysteries get solved. Once holes started appearing in melons, and close examination revealed tooth marks. I thought deer or raccoons might have caused them. But then it dawned on me that the neighbor's cat had been spending a lot of time in the melon patch. Coyotes are known to like melons, so why not cats?

Many of the things that happened in gardens were not surprising or mysterious, simply enjoyable. There was no mystery about the flattened and disheveled state of a catnip patch by the cat-eaten melon bed. I liked turning a sprinkler on a bed and seeing a goldfinch flock descend to drink from the wet leaves. I liked finding black swallowtail butterfly chrysalises on dill or parsley plants, and wolf spiders sunning their eggs at the mouths of their tunnels under tomato plants. I liked of the cleverness of the big black bees that frequented *Nicotiana* flowers: unable to reach into the narrow corolla tubes, they got nectar by piercing the trumpet-shaped flowers at the base. One spring, I especially liked looking out the window and seeing four black-headed grosbeaks, two western tanagers, a lazuli bunting, a golden-crowned sparrow, a white-crowned sparrow, a Wilson's warbler, a yellow-rumped warbler, two linnets, and a robin in the garden at once.

Most of the above creatures were benefiting the garden by eating pests or weeds, the kind of relationship that stimulated my Yellow Cab vision of harmony. They weren't benefiting it enough to stop the pests and weeds. If they did, they wouldn't be around anymore, since there'd be nothing for them to eat. The harmony of songbirds in a garden depends on the disharmony of pests and weeds in it, a disharmony that arises in its turn from the garden's disturbances.

Harmony from disturbance doesn't sound reasonable, but it does reflect what science has learned about the planet's workings in the past few centuries. We can no longer regard earth as an orderly hierarchy as medieval and Renaissance savants did, or as a smoothly functioning machine, as Enlightenment philosophes did. The fossil record discloses a biosphere that has existed for over three billion years by being disorderly and rough. Things get disturbed all the time—mass extinctions wipe out entire biotas—but, interestingly—and surprisingly—no instance of *universal* chaos and destruction has occurred so far.

—*Country Journal*, August 1981

leapers and creepers

bay area frogs and toads

Walking in the hills one hot April afternoon, I happened on a nearly evaporated puddle containing newly hatched tadpoles. Since I had a newly emptied Peet's Coffee cup in my hand, a puddle-to-cup tadpole transfer occurred before mature reflection could intervene. Amphibians always have fascinated me. The way their strange shapes and colors materialize out of earth and water seems magical. But childhood attempts to keep them as pets had been smelly failures, and if I'd found a full puddle on the way back to my car, I would have released the tadpoles. But I didn't find one, so I arrived home with a dozen or so pinhead-sized brown larvae in an inch of diluted adobe mud and cappuccino foam.

I dumped them in a small aquarium and sprinkled some TerraMin Baby Fish Food for Egglayers in the water. They went after it as though they'd evolved particularly to eat "fishmeal, torula dried yeast, ground brown rice, potato products, wheat gluten, dehulled soybean meal, and natural and artificial colors," swimming upside down to suck it into swelling paunches. Their enthusiasm for my largesse was flattering and their vitality and adaptability were gratifying at a time when frog news generally concerns imminent death from pollution, climate change, and habitat loss.

When the water started to smell, I changed it with a turkey baster, but that was all I did in the way of tadpole cultivation. They responded with a complexity that seemed disproportionate to my kitchen technology. They developed daily and with bewildering diversity, displaying a range of genetic variation that probably contributes to adaptive strategies in the wild. Some stayed dark brown and pinhead sized. Some stayed dark brown but grew within weeks to sunflower seed–sized. Others turned greenish or beige and also grew quickly.

Hind legs soon appeared on the large brown tadpoles, then on the green and beige ones. Tails shrank and front legs appeared. By early June, four-legged individuals lurked near the aquarium lid, ready to bounce halfway across the room when I lifted it at feeding or basting time. Even the pinheads had begun to metamorphose into miniatures of their larger siblings. By the Fourth of July, I had released the bouncing brood in the backyard, not really expecting to see them again given Berkeley's house cat, raccoon, opossum, skunk, jay, and crow populations.

In August, however, I started finding half dollar–sized frogs in flowerpots, some dark brown or greenish, some pinkish or mottled green and beige. During the first fall rains, when the local termite nests produced their sparkle-winged wedding flights, happy croaks issued from the shrubbery. The frogs were such an interesting presence that my wife and I optimistically built a three-foot-wide "vernal pool" for them beside the tool shed, hoping they might breed.

My backyard brood belonged to the West Coast's most common and adaptable species, which used to be called the Pacific tree frog (*Hyla*) but was renamed the Pacific chorus frog (*Pseudacris*) because it is more like the chorus frogs elsewhere in North America and less like the tree frogs. Chorus frogs usually sing on the ground while tree frogs sometimes sing in trees. (North American frogs all breed on the ground, although some tropical frogs breed in trees.) Anyway, I've never seen a Pacific chorus frog in a tree, so the name change seems justifiable.

More resistant to pollution and habitat modification than other species—as I discovered with my Peet's Coffee waifs—Pacific chorus frogs will breed in most kinds of freshwater. They lived everywhere in the Bay Area before urbanization destroyed much of their habitat. They've even counterattacked against growth in some cases, invading ornamental lakes in gated communities, disturbing New Economy slumbers with clamorous water sports. Philip Northen, professor of biology at Sonoma State University and a frog expert, told me that he gets phone calls from subdividers and property managers asking how to exterminate frogs. "I just tell them they should learn to love nature," he said.

Pacific chorus frog calls *are* amazingly loud, as anyone who has heard a breeding pond knows. (In a sense, they are the calls heard around the world, since Hollywood has used them as sound effects in thousands of movies—they should get royalties.) What is less well-known is that their calls are not just chaotic screeching but a "language" that organizes breeding. Northen said that their vocabulary's function is not well understood but that male Pacific chorus frogs make five kinds of calls, each adapted to particular functions in attracting females and repelling rival males.

These pond calls are distinct from ones they make on land, which are even less well understood. Pacific chorus frogs spend most of their lives on land, passing the dry season in ground squirrel burrows, wood rat dens, and other refuges. Their terrestrial adaptability is as remarkable as their aquatic one. When I lived in Round Valley in northeast Mendocino County, chorus frogs inhabited a tin-roofed storage shed during summers when ambient temperature often climbed into the 90s.

A melodious chirping sometimes accompanies chorus frog screeching in breeding ponds. This is the call of western toads (*Bufo boreas*), the Bay Area's second most adaptable species. They have similar ways of life, staying in burrows and other refuges in dry times and moving to breeding waters in late winter and spring. The western toad's black tadpoles are easily distinguished from chorus frogs' grayish or brownish ones, and they are often in ponds or creeks after the chorus tadpoles have metamorphosed and left, since toads tend to breed later. Baby toads are blackish too, but as they mature they become greenish or brownish gray, with light dorsal stripes and warts that are often rusty colored. The warts, and parotid glands behind the eyes, exude a milky toxin that can poison attackers, although some determined predators, such as raccoons and ravens, have learned to avoid the skin and eat what's inside. Growing to three times chorus frog size, western toads are more conspicuous as they emerge at twilight to forage. They can cover a lot of ground, creeping as well as leaping, and will attack formidable prey, including wasps and scorpions.

Pacific chorus frogs and western toads are the Bay Area's most numerous anurans now, but in the past the largest native frog, the California red-legged frog, may have been even more so. The species likes to breed in big wetlands, a habitat more available in the past. Mark Jennings, a herpetologist at the California Academy of Sciences, researched late-nineteenth-century commercial red-legged frog exploitation. He said that California diners consumed the legs of an estimated 60,000 to 80,000 a year, until the wild "froggery" collapsed after a record capture of 118,000 in 1895. The industry turned to "ranching" imported bull-frogs, and escapees hastened the native frogs' decline by preying on them and preempting breeding habitat. The California red-legged frog declined so markedly that in 1996 it became the first Bay Area anuran to be federally listed as a threatened species.

Another native anuran, the foothill yellow-legged frog, *Rana boylii*, spends its life around permanently flowing streams, not a common Bay Area habitat now. A medium-sized, mottled, tan or grayish frog, it is usually seen only briefly as it jumps into the water or hides under a rock. It is heard even less than it is seen and was once thought to vocalize very little, which would make sense, given its noisy stream habitat. Professor Northen and a student recently discovered, however, that male yellow-legged frogs call to females underwater, where sound carries better than in air, and that they do so volubly. Northen said that male yellow-leggeds have seven calls that they use to attract females and repel rivals.

The western spadefoot toad, *Spea hammondii*, can be quite noisy; its call has been compared to sawing wood. People here very seldom hear it because the stout, cat-eyed little creature lives only in isolated areas along the Central Valley's western margin. And unlike other Bay Area anurans, which remain active through the year if weather is not too hot or cold, spadefoots spend eight to nine months a year dormant in soil, emerging only to breed and feed when a profuse spell of warm rain occurs. They may not emerge at all in dry years.

Mainly a desert species, the spadefoot is a relict of drier times in the Bay Area. Nature documentary makers like desert spadefoots because they breed explosively in puddles left by summer thunderstorms. In that situation, they can develop from eggs to baby toads in three weeks, larger tadpoles supplementing their diet by eating smaller ones. Not sur-prisingly, they are fast eaters. A spadefoot can gulp prey equivalent to 11 percent of its body mass in one meal.

Summer cloudbursts are rare here, and knowledge about local spade-foot breeding is limited. Robert Stebbins, an emeritus professor at UC–Berkeley who has been observing local amphibians since the 1940s, said that the species is most active from April to June, breeding in streams or ponds as well as ephemeral pools. Mark Jennings said they may breed after fall rains as well. Larry Serpa, a Nature Conservancy biologist, found spadefoot tadpoles in stock ponds east of Henry Coe State Park.

He raised them on fish food and then returned the babies to their natal pools, where they immediately burrowed into the mud with the spade-like structures on their hind legs for which they are named, disappearing within a half hour.

A flexible lot, Bay Area frogs and toads resisted civilization better than the mighty condors, elk, and grizzlies. Urbanization, wetland destruction, and stream diversion reduced some populations, but irrigation and water impoundments may have provided new habitat for others. Anurans remained fairly common here into the mid-twentieth century; their main decline here seems to have come after 1970. David Wake, a leading herpetologist and professor of biology at UC–Berkeley, sadly watched western toads and Pacific chorus frogs dwindle in the Oakland and Berkeley Hills. "I haven't seen a toad there in years," he said. Chorus frogs still call in Tilden Regional Park, but Steve Bobzien, regional services coordinator for the East Bay Regional Park District (EBRPD), does not have records of western toads in the Berkeley or Oakland Hills for the past several years. "There's a strong indication that toads are losing part of their range," he said.

Ironically, the Bay Area's federally listed anuran, the California red-legged frog, is not the rarest species here, remaining widespread if inconspicuous in creeks, stock ponds, and wetlands. Red-legged frogs have low-pitched calls and spend most of their lives in or around water so people encounter them less than chorus frogs or toads. The species's behavior is unpredictable, as I've discovered at Mount Diablo State Park. Chorus frogs and toads breed in the same ponds and streams there year after year; red-legged frogs appear and disappear mysteriously. I hiked along Pine Creek in Mount Diablo for years before seeing one; then I saw a pair in the creek one spring. That summer, a pool farther upstream was suddenly full of big tadpoles. The next summer, it was empty again. A few summers later, it was full again. There was even a red-legged frog in it, although I got only a glimpse before it hid under a rock. On Wall Ridge above the creek, I often hiked past a muddy stock pond that showed no signs of frogs. Then, one autumn, hundreds of half-grown ones leapt into the water at my approach. But I never saw frogs there again.

Although spadefoot toads and foothill yellow-legged frogs are sparse here, they aren't listed, because populations not known to be at risk exist elsewhere. I've heard of only a few streams in the East and South Bay where sizable populations of yellow-legged frogs survive, although they may be doing better in the North Bay. The spadefoot toad's local situation is even more precarious, since its main population at Corral Hollow is under pressure from increased traffic, off-road vehicles, and pet collecting. "Spadefoot toads are cute," Mark Jennings told me. Larry Serpa said the spadefoot population east of Henry Coe is "pretty minimal."

Urban sprawl and its attendant habitat destruction, water pollution, and traffic are obvious factors in anuran decline. But the creatures have dwindled even in natural areas. Thin-skinned amphibians may be particularly vulnerable to what Robert Stebbins called a "witch's brew" of airborne urban and agribusiness chemicals, as suggested by population declines in places where prevailing winds concentrate it, such as the Sierra Nevada. Jennings said that medfly spraying in the 1980s may have impacted Bay Area anurans seriously. Introduced fish like trout, bass, and perch (even the little mosquito fish distributed by insect abatement agencies) can reduce breeding native anurans. Studies in Oregon suggested that increased ultraviolet radiation caused by atmospheric ozone depletion could sterilize eggs—although Jennings said that other studies failed to duplicate those results. Warming and drying climate caused by the global greenhouse effect will not benefit species that need cool, moist habitat.

The best hope for anurans lies in parks and other protected lands, and management agencies are looking at ways of helping them. But doubts about causes of the decline muddy the waters. Stebbins said that the East Bay Municipal Utility District restored a red-legged frog population when it fenced cattle out of a creek. Livestock trampling and overgrazing certainly degrade riparian and wetland habitat. On the other hand, Steve Bobzien said that cattle don't seem to be a major frog-limiting factor on EBRPD land. He said that 75 of the 265 ponds on EBRPD property support red-legged frogs, 65 of them with breeding populations, and that the most productive ones weren't fenced. Gary Fellers, a research biologist at Point Reyes National Seashore, said that red-legged frogs inhabited most of the stock ponds at the seashore's pastoral-zone dairy farms and that more lived on grazed lands than others. He thought cows and frogs could coexist with proper management to protect riparian vegetation and control silting.

Red-legged frogs can travel as much as a mile to and from breeding waters during winter rains. Fellers was conducting radio tracking studies of their movements to better understand their relationship with cattle.

He also planned to fit frogs with infrared lights so he could study their nocturnal behavior. I asked him how he attached gadgets to frogs. "We have little belts that we put on them," he said. "You just straighten their legs out and slip them on."

Everybody at least agrees that bullfrogs and exotic fish threaten native anurans. Bobzien told me that EBRPD has restored some red-legged frog populations by removing bullfrogs and exotic fish from ponds, and "redesigning" the ponds to favor native species. Other park agencies have implemented similar measures. Agencies seemed less clear about conserving the four nonlisted species, however. Bobzien said that EBRPD was trying to link protection of its one substantial foothill yellow-legged frog population with a steelhead trout restoration project. A stream with water capable of supporting steelhead breeding presumably can support yellow-legged frog breeding. The main strategy for protecting the other three species—Pacific chorus frogs, western toads, and spadefoot toads—seemed to be simply preserving as much habitat as possible.

Bay Area frogs and toads are definitely down in the twenty-first century. But that doesn't mean they're out. Anurans are old hands at survival. Fossils show that they appeared in the Jurassic period, the middle of the dinosaur age, and remained abundant through the next 200 million years, while thousands of bigger, smarter kinds of animals perished in mass extinctions. As I found at Mount Diablo, anuran demographics can be deceptive. Populations burgeon or shrink mysteriously and may reappear where they seemed long gone. The larger species begin to breed when they are two or three years old and have relatively long life spans. California red-legged frogs can live up to eight years in the wild, and western toads have been known to inhabit the same garden for a decade or more. Chorus frogs have shorter lives but breed faster.

The survival of anurans in remoter parts of the Bay Area doesn't really compensate for the absence of chorus frog calls on a rainy night, or toads snapping up bugs on a summer evening. (A book published in 1961 estimated the value of a single garden toad's insect control at up to fifty dollars a year, which might make it about ten times that in the twenty-first century's real estate market.) It is not impossible to reestablish native anurans in suburbs. I've seen native frogs and toads living in an Ohio backyard, whose owners told me that American toads, *Bufo americanus*, had been returning to breed in a pond there for several years. But it's not easy, as I found with my Pacific chorus frogs. It's also illegal in California, for various environmental reasons—although a hard law to enforce.

Anyway, we were overoptimistic with our vernal pool. One night I heard raccoons yammering and splashing in it. The next morning, I found that all the rocks I'd used to floor it had been turned over and piled in the middle, with proprietary scat on top. Still, at least one of the frogs—a big brown one—survived in our tool shed for over a year. We'd see him sometimes on the top shelf and hear him croaking even in dry weather.

—*Bay Nature*, April–June 2002

megafauna by the bay

If you rode a time machine a million years back to a Bay Area ridge, you might think that the contraption wasn't working. You would glimpse a bay through oak and pine trees like today's, and a passing songbird or squirrel would resemble living species. Roars and snarls from the canyon below might sound like a motocross. But the illusion of modernity would fade as you heard something coming up the hill. Trail motorcycles don't breathe in deep, hoarse pants.

When it came into sight, you might not know what to think. You might think it was a bear, since it would have a similar massive, plantigrade presence. But it would have much longer legs than a modern bear's, and a shorter muzzle. Whatever you thought, you'd probably be scared, and with reason, since the beast, now known as the short-faced bear (*Arctodus simus*), was not only very big but probably as swiftly predatory as it looked.

More roars from below, however, would suggest that *Arctodus* was in flight from something, and its departure would be as swift as its arrival. If curiosity overcame fright and you went downhill to investigate, you might find that a pair of saber-toothed cats and a pack of dire wolves were too busy squabbling over the camel carcass from which they'd driven *Arctodus* to notice you. You might justifiably be more wary of some watching mammoths, perhaps like today's elephants in getting testy around predators. And the numbers of waiting scavengers—foxes, coyotes, vultures, condors, and even larger birds called teratorns—might unnerve you. With so much happening, you might not notice that even more beasts were in sight—ground sloths, horses, peccaries, and musk oxen, as well as ungulates not unlike today's black-tailed deer and pronghorns.

Although most of these creatures seem exotic now, we know they lived here because their bones remain. In fact, the Bay Area contains North America's best collection of bones from the time when they lived, from 1.2 million to five hundred thousand years ago. In 1936, teenage fossil hunters found a large bone deposit in a gravel pit near the Alameda County town of Irvington near Fremont. Because of its abundance and diversity, paleontologists refer to the site as the "type locality" for the period, which they call the Irvingtonian age.

Despite its importance, the Irvington site isn't well-known even in the Bay Area, perhaps partly because Los Angeles County's fossil-rich La Brea Tar Pits have eclipsed it. The tar pits' scientific value is similar: they are the type locality for the Rancholabrean age, which directly followed the Irvingtonian. (Both were part of the Pleistocene epoch, which lasted from 1.8 million to fifteen thousand years ago.) But the La Brea animals' sensational death—trapped in natural tar deposits—made them world famous, whereas the Irvingtonian bones' gradual deposition in streambeds was more normal. The George Page Museum in Los Angles County lavishly displays La Brea's fossils to the public. UC–Berkeley's Museum of Paleontology mostly keeps Irvington's in drawers (where most fossil bones end up).

Famous or not, both ages are typical of evolution's past 200 million years in that assemblages of big animals—herbivores, carnivores, and scavengers—dominated them. Biologists call these assemblages megafaunas. Dinosaur megafaunas prevailed until 65 million years ago; then mammals replaced them, although living megafaunas also include some large dinosaur relatives—birds and reptiles. About fifteen thousand years ago, however, diverse megafaunas began to disappear, although relict ones, like those of East Africa or Yellowstone, remain. The causes of this mass extinction aren't well understood, although human population growth undoubtedly contributed. The effects are even less well understood but are even more important, because they will affect the planet's future.

Ecologists worry about the long-term effects of losing megafaunas because the plants and animals alive today coevolved with them. Daniel Janzen, a biologist who works in Central America, notes that many plants have large, hard, tasty fruits and other features adapted for big mammals like horses, camels, ground sloths, and mammoths to eat. He thinks that many of these plants have become scarce since megafauna disappeared because the mammals that lived with them helped to spread and germinate their seeds by eating them. As such plants become scarcer or go extinct, many other animals and plants that interact with them (as pollinators, browsers, nesters, epiphytes. and so on) may die out too.

In the Costa Rican national park where he works, Janzen has tried to restore some megafaunal influence by allowing controlled browsing by livestock such as horses (wild horse species inhabited the region before the mass extinction), which enthusiastically eat fruits of native trees like *guanacaste* and *jicaro*. Many other biologists are thinking about mega-fauna restoration, including reintroduction of native large wild animals as well as domestic ones. Some dream of resurrecting extinct species such as mammoths by cloning them from fossil DNA.

Is some megafauna restoration possible in a megalopolis like the Bay Area? To be sure, the Bay Area is an unusual megalopolis in having as much remnant megafauna as it does—not only deer but predators in-cluding mountain lions, bobcats, coyotes, foxes, eagles, and falcons. And that is not to mention the marine megafauna here, which is world class, on par with East Africa's land megafauna. No coasts outside the poles have as diverse a marine megafauna as North America's Pacific one, and the Bay Area is at the center of it. Although decimated in the nineteenth century, the known historic species have recovered to some extent with the exception of the Steller's sea cow, which hunters exterminated a few decades after it was discovered. Still, like Africa, the Pacific is not easy of access, and humans are physically less adapted to admire gray whales and orcas than elephants and lions.

We are lucky to have what we do in the way of land animals, a result of the local tradition of preserving public open space. But could we have more? Of course, an Irvington-like fauna of more than a dozen large wild herbivore species supporting as many big predator and scavenger species would need more space than our largest wild lands could provide. Still, Bay Area woodlands, chaparral, and grasslands co-evolved with such faunas, and restoring them to some extent could help ameliorate some of the problems in sustaining those ecosystems. Oaks might reproduce better, for example, if more big kinds of animals were spreading acorns, and fire might be less of a threat if there were more browsers and grazers.

A more diverse megafauna would certainly make local wild lands more exciting. Although we don't want big wild animals roaming the streets (a few occasionally do roam the streets, too excitingly in some cases), we have an affinity for them, since we coevolved with them too. As Thoreau wistfully wrote in 1850s Massachusetts, where even deer were extirpated: "We need to witness our own limits transgressed, and some life pasturing freely where we never wander. . . . We must be refreshed by the sight of inexhaustible vigor, vast and titanic features."

If we were to restore some native megafauna to the Bay Area, what kinds might we hope to see "pasturing freely"? The short-faced bear, *Arctodus*, is an unlikely prospect because it has no close living relatives, but several other Irvingtonian species do. An Irvingtonian-age cheetah left its bones in the Sacramento Valley. Cheetahs lived throughout the West then, and they may have evolved on this continent before migrating to the Old World. Paleontologists suspect the fleet cats may be a reason why pronghorns can run faster than any living North American predator, forty miles an hour.

Cheetahs haven't lived here for at least fifteen thousand years, however, which raises the question of exactly what an ecologically functional Bay Area megafauna might be. Would it be the animals that lived here when humans first arrived, probably between forty thousand and twelve thousand years ago? Would it be the animals that lived here in historical times? Could there be some kind of "ideal" megafauna for this region—maybe a bit closer to the Irvingtonian's than today's—that land managers might try to approximate?

We don't know exactly when most of the big Pleistocene mammals disappeared from California, but most were gone by the time Europeans arrived. The California grizzly was the only real giant, and some big animals common elsewhere in North America were absent or scarce here. Bison, which had invaded North America from Eurasia during the Rancholabrean age, inhabited only the northeast corner of California in historical times. Wolves, the continent's top modern predators, the only ones to habitually tackle bison, don't seem to have been numerous in the Bay Area during historical times, although reports of them exist. Besides grizzlies, our historically common megafauna were on the medium-to-small side of the prehistoric scale.

It impressed European explorers anyway. A journal from Sir Francis Drake's expedition described thousands of "very large and fat deer," in

1579, probably at Point Reyes. Two centuries later, in 1772, Pedro Fages reported "plentiful game such as deer, antelope, elk, bear" in the East Bay, while Juan Crespi saw grizzlies and deer in the Oakland estuary and "many antelopes and tracks of bears" in the San Benito Valley. Grizzlies thrived on Spanish cattle as carcasses stripped of their salable hides dotted valleys. A French explorer, A. Duhaut Ceilly, found bears so abundant in 1827 that "without going farther than five or six leagues from San Francisco, they are often seen in herds." A few years later, Richard Henry Dana, a Harvard student visiting the Bay Area as a sailor in the hide trade, found elk almost as common as the Drake expedition had.

"We came to anchor near the mouth of the bay," he wrote in his classic memoir, *Two Years before the Mast*, "under a high and beautifully sloping hill, upon which hundreds and hundreds of red deer, and the stag, with his high branching antlers, were bounding about, looking at us for a moment, and then starting off, affrighted at the noises which we made for the purpose of seeing the variety of their beautiful attitudes and motions."

The abundance didn't last long after American homesteaders replaced Mexican hide barons. Ranchers and market hunters killed grizzlies, elk, and pronghorns for meat, skins, and tallow. Miners killed condors just for their quills, used to store gold dust. By the 1890s, all these large animals were gone from the Bay Area, along with the gray whales, sea otters, elephants seals, and fur seals that had abounded a century before. And while most of the marine mammals have returned to some degree, fewer of the land mammals have.

On the other hand, with our accidental or deliberate help, other kinds of wild or semiwild animals invaded, filling ecological niches vacated by extirpated natives. Mustang herds grew so large that vaqueros massacred them during droughts to save cattle forage. They had disappeared by the 1900s, but feral domestic pigs and cattle survived in the hills. In the 1920s, landowners near Monterey released Eurasian wild boars for hunting, and, with sows bearing litters of a dozen piglets a year, they had spread to twenty-eight California counties by 1985. In the 1960s, the California Department of Fish and Game introduced wild turkeys as game animals. Absent historically, turkeys were common in Pleistocene California, although of a different species than today. Weighing the same as California condors, turkeys dominate the ground-dwelling avian niche. Their gobbling has become a normal spring sound in local wild lands—even in towns.

Pigs and turkeys have pervaded Bay Area wild lands since I started frequenting them in the 1970s. Then I went to Henry Coe State Park to see them. Now I can watch turkeys' private lives up close at Mount Diablo, where the mating season renders them oblivious to intruders. Tom turkeys make theories of birds' close relationship to dinosaurs seems glaringly obvious: they are strikingly colorful in their breeding finery—bright blue and red heads, gold and bronze tail fans. On one April day, I watched from a few feet away as trios of toms displayed before hens. (A coyote pair also looked on hopefully from a discreet distance.) A trio would approach one of the smaller, drab hens, which would make soft, flutelike calls. This would inspire the toms to gobble in unison, with such force that it shook their bodies. The toms would then turn around and strut away, spreading their tail fans, enticing the hen to follow them. This eventually would lead to mating, although I didn't see it. But the results are there: turkey nests and broods are common.

Pigs are less confiding at Mount Diablo because the state keeps trying to trap them out. The pigs keep coming back, however, and their presence is often evident where they've rooted up the ground. When I first started seeing them there, they were the brown, hairy feral kind, small and timid. Later I started seeing more of the black, furry wild boars, which are bigger and bolder. I've seen families of them curiously investigating the wire cage traps. (I've also seen turkey flocks entering set traps to eat the bait, although not with sufficient enthusiasm to spring the trap doors. Evidently they prefer wild foods to pheromone-soaked corn.)

In the 1970s, the state legislature told the Department of Fish and Game to restore historically native species where feasible. Tule elk, a subspecies of the genus *Cervus* (which entered North America from Eurasia in the Rancholabrean age), were the biggest native ungulates in the historic Bay Area, the ones Drake and Dana admired. Although hunting reduced the state's population to a few individuals in the southern San Joaquin Valley, the elk recovered under protection, and small groups from those refuges multiplied after reintroduction to fenced Bay Area sites at Tomales Point in Point Reyes National Seashore, Concord Naval Weapons Station, and Grizzly Island in the delta.

The Tomales Point herd grew in two decades from eight cows and two bulls in 1978 to more than four hundred. In 1999, the Park Service moved twenty-eight animals to the seashore's Phil Burton Wilderness Area, where hikers can see them roaming freely. Fish and Game released elk near Mount Hamilton southeast of San Jose, where they expanded into three herds, one staying in that vicinity, one moving north to San Antonio Reservoir, the other east toward the San Joaquin Valley. Tule elk restoration has succeeded because the species is prolific and adaptable, able to browse on exotic weeds like plantain as well as native food plants. But attempts to reintroduce other native species have been more problematic.

No living North American mammal is more native than the graceful pronghorn, which is not an antelope as explorers assumed but the last survivor of a group, the antilocaprids, that has inhabited this continent for at least 15 million years. (No antelopes are native to the Americas.) Pronghorns have recovered from near extinction in much of the West, but little of their valley grassland habitat remains in the Bay Area, and they are less prolific than elk. So although Fish and Game released some at Mount Hamilton at the same time as elk, the result was inconclusive. Some drifted north toward Livermore but then disappeared. But I heard that others had stayed near Mount Hamilton and grown to a herd of about forty on private land.

With help from a local pilot, I flew for a few minutes over the ranch where they were said to live. Focusing binoculars from a small plane is hard, but I saw a scattering of beige specks near a group of larger beige-and-brown ones. I could tell the larger specks were elk, so I guessed that the smaller specks were pronghorns. A herd of forty isn't many compared to the forty-fold elk increase at Tomales Point, however. Point Reyes is the only other Bay Area site where pronghorns might be restored, but there are no historical records of them there, so restoration is controversial.

Condor restoration here is also problematic since the closest population is on the central coast. The Ventana Wilderness Society began reintroducing condors to Big Sur in 1996 and released more at Pinnacles National Monument in 2003. If this population grows to the goal of fifty birds, condors might once again inhabit the Bay Area, but it could take awhile. Condors are very social, and central coast birds prefer to roam south to visit the population around Santa Barbara. Gaps in the ridgelines between the Bay Area and central coast also work against northward movement because they weaken the thermal air currents condors like to ride. Some condors have appeared in the Bay Area in recent years, but only briefly.

All the attention that condors get seems a little unfair to their smaller cousins, turkey vultures. We reward them for thriving and cleaning up road kills by ignoring and rather despising them. But the Bay Area would be diminished without turkey vultures soaring overhead, and the way they manage to do it virtually everywhere, despite all the urbanization, is admirable. I don't understand how they do manage. Their nesting and feeding habits aren't so different from condors' and they are also quite social. While turkeys are doing their mating rituals on the slopes of Mount Diablo in spring, I sometimes see vultures doing theirs on ridgetops. A group of birds will land and strut about, evidently males trying to impress a female, although it's hard to tell because they aren't sexually dimorphic. Turkey vultures can seem pretty casual about where they lay their eggs—sometimes just on the ground in the woods. On the other hand, finding a turkey vulture's ground nest is not easy. The species seems to have a talent for fading into the background when not soaring overhead, perhaps one key to its success.

I can't mention vultures without bringing in the big-three raptors: ospreys, bald eagles, and golden eagles. Osprey restoration after the DDT population crash of the 1950s has been so successful that it's seldom mentioned now. But I remember the lift I felt when, having lived away from the Bay Area for awhile, I walked the Bear Valley Trail at Point Reyes again, heard squeaky noises from the big Douglas firs overhead, and realized there were osprey nests up there. Bald eagle restoration seems to have lagged in the Bay Area—at least I've never seen one here—but since the California population is growing, maybe I will. The Bay Area's world-class golden eagle population has dodged DDT and ground squirrel eradication campaigns, although wind farms aren't doing it any good. I've seen a lot of them in the South Bay ridge lands, usually soaring but sometimes running around on the ground like chickens. They're a regular if infrequent sight at Mount Diablo. One day, walking on Wall Ridge in the adjacent regional park, I saw a flock of city rock doves feeding on the cattle pasture there, and, on a power line above, a pair of eagles. The next time I walked that way, I found little piles of pigeon feathers here and there.

As of now, there are no further plans to restore native megafauna in or near the Bay Area. California grizzly restoration in wilderness areas has enthusiasts, but they don't suggest releasing half-ton bears here. Self-restoration of natives is another possibility, however. Jules Evens's field guide to Point Reyes described the river otter as extinct in the seashore in 1988, so I had trouble believing my eyes when I saw a pair cavorting at Five Ponds in 1996. But I saw them again in 1997, and the species seems to have returned to Point Reyes permanently. Maybe their marine cousins, sea otters, will come back to Drakes Bay, one of their population centers before their nineteenth-century extirpation. Elephant seals have returned on their own, so why not sea otters? Planned designation of Drakes Estero as the state's first marine wilderness area could help with that, as designation of the Phil Burton Wilderness in the national seashore doubtless helped river otters. That is what "wilderness" means: a place for wild beasts, *wildeor* in Anglo-Saxon. (Congress designated a 141-acre wilderness on parts of the Farallon Islands in 1974, but not in the water around them.)

Another self-restoration candidate entered the limelight in May 2003, when newspapers reported a black bear raiding a Dumpster of the Point Reyes Youth Hostel near Limantour Beach, the first Marin bear sighting in a century. Further sightings occurred through the summer in a dozen sites from Tomales Bay State Park to Kirby Cove on the Golden Gate, and DNA hair and scat samples showed that the bear was a male with a taste for fruit, seeds, and paper towels. Biologists guessed he had come from Sonoma County. It's not clear that black bears occurred in Marin County historically. A letter to the *San Francisco Chronicle* maintained that only grizzlies did, a view held by Tracy I. Storer and Lloyd P. Tevis in their 1955 classic *California Grizzly*. On the other hand, a report of several bears clownishly invading the Marin town of Olema in the 1860s sounds more like the smaller species (seldom weighing more than three hundred pounds) than the fearsome grizzly. West Marin's conifer and hardwood forest would be suitable black bear habitat.

Black bears don't seem to have lived in the drier East and South Bays historically, or in the central and south coast generally. Grizzlies may have excluded them, although the two species coexisted in the Sierra and north coast. After grizzly extirpation from the state in the 1920s, black bears spread from the southern Sierra through the Coast Range north to the Santa Cruz Mountains. Changes in hunting laws and habitat allowed a tripling of the population after the 1980s, so the species may wander into Bay Area wildlands from the south as well as the north.

The arrival in northeast California of a wolf from the restored Rocky Mountain population raised another possibility for self-reintroduction, although the Bay Area probably lacks enough wild land and large wild prey for a wolf population. Still, wolves are so wide ranging that their occasional occurrence can't be ruled out, although ranchers' reaction to the possibility has not been positive.

Ranchers aren't the only ones to view megafauna restoration with alarm. Some environmentalists see large introduced animals, whether native or exotic, as threats to ecosystems already hammered by humans. Think of Hilda and Alphonse, the gluttonous black bears from Phil Frank's comic strip *Farley*, descending on Marin's painstakingly restored salmon and steelhead runs. Turkeys compete for acorns and other foods, and may eat threatened small animals like red-legged frogs. Native plant enthusiasts wring their hands as wild boars root up hillsides in search of food.

Biologists and land managers see boars as the chief villains and often speak of them as their nineteenth-century counterparts spoke of coyotes and lions. *Farley*'s bears are likable Dumpster layabouts; its boars are nouveau riche, resource-guzzling "Watt Hogs." I'm not sure that boars are all bad, though. They may have a part to play. For most of California vegetation's evolution, as animals such as pronghorns, elk, and deer grazed or browsed it, others such as mastodons, and ground sloths "plowed" it, seeking roots, bulbs, truffles, and other buried foods. As Daniel Janzen observes, the plants are adapted to such treatment and in some cases depend on it. When those species disappeared about fifteen thousand years ago, grizzlies continued to occupy the rooting niche. Explorers wrote of entire ridges dug up by bears.

Now boars occupy the niche. In remote areas like Henry Coe State Park, sizable boar populations coexist with grasslands and savannas that retain many native plant species. Elsewhere, boars root up mats of exotic grasses and forbs left by intensive ranching. This is unsightly, like one recently rooted swale I examined. Formerly thick with exotic hay grasses like timothy, it now contained mostly exotic weeds—sow thistle, milk thistle, Canada thistle, and black mustard—with some native tarweeds mixed in. Yet, on the drier slopes just above the swale, where the boars had rooted the slopes down to bare soil, the plants that remained were almost all natives, including purple needlegrass, wild rye, biscuitroot, soaproot, blue-eyed grass, mule's ear sunflowers, tarweeds, and oak seedlings. In contrast, exotic wild oats predominated on surrounding hillsides. I don't understand how this happened—but there it was.

Boars affect small wildlife as well as vegetation, since they'll eat anything they can catch. But I haven't perceived any marked impact on other species, in contrast to the situation at Point Reyes, where population explosions of exotic fallow and axis deer that competed for the browsing niche noticeably decreased the numbers of native blacktailed deer, even possibly of smaller herbivores. Boars don't compete with large native rooters, since none remain here except possibly black bears. Biologists worry about boars impacting bears in Appalachia, but they coexist in wildlands throughout Eurasia. Visiting national parks in Thailand (where I saw a sun bear sitting in a tree like Baloo in *The Jungle Book*), I was surprised at park administrations' positive attitude to boars, especially since so many more charismatic species live there. One park had a kiosk devoted to boar behavior, including that they sometimes build huts of branches for shelter during the rainy season. I've never seen *that*. (*Farley*'s Watt Hogs live in monster homes.)

Mature wild boars definitely are not cute (young ones are), but they are magnificent beasts, leggy and agile in the woods. Indeed, the gregarious, prolific Old World species would be a more appropriate mascot for present-day California than the solitary, slow-breeding grizzly. It would take just one letter to change UC–Berkeley's Golden Bears into its Golden Boars. That won't happen, of course, and wild boar rooting is certainly no ecological panacea in today's wildlands. Its erosive potential worries harried water managers. Interestingly, however, there's not much we can do to stop boars from influencing the ecosystem. They're more a part of it now than we are.

The boar situation has a corollary that may represent a missed opportunity. The Irvingtonian fauna included a peccary of the genus *Platygonus* that probably rooted for food. *Platygonus* was long considered extinct, but in 1972, biologists in the remote Paraguayan Gran Chaco forest discovered a living genus, *Catagonus*, very like it. Introducing *Catagonus* here might have helped a rare, dwindling species to survive while filling the rooting niche with more manageable animals than the wild boars. But the boars now fill the niche, a lesson in the downside of careless meddling with nature.

Given such difficulties, could what we have now in the Bay Area be called a functional megafauna? Nobody sees today's unplanned mélange of natives and exotics as ideal. Still, I think Bay Area wildlands are better for the big animals that survive in them, although that's hard to prove in light of our limited understanding of their long-term ecological and evolutionary role. My own experience in decades of local hiking suggests that they enliven their environment. That may be because such places are among the most remote and undisturbed, but not necessarily. I've seen more biological exuberance around the elk at Tomales Point and Limantour than on many walks through the more remote but elk-less southern part of Phil Burton Wilderness.

One October day in 1994, I saw three long-tailed weasels at Tomales Point, more than I've seen elsewhere in one day. I also saw a burrowing owl, which I hadn't seen elsewhere at Point Reyes. One foggy afternoon after elk reintroduction at Limantour, every coyote bush seemed to have a young rabbit under it, and one bush had a coyote under it, the first I'd seen there. That August, I witnessed a mass migration of quail there, hundreds trooping up an elk-browsed hillside. I've seen quail all over the Bay Area, of course, but not hundreds in one place. Naturalists have often remarked on an abundance of smaller animals around big ones, suggesting that they improve habitat for all by renewing and diversifying vegetation with their activities. Daniel Janzen writes that landscapes "moderately and patchily browsed" by a variety of big animals "may be more like those before megafaunal extinction than were those present at the time of the Spanish conquest."

On the other hand, Janzen also observes that large megafaunas may limit some smaller creatures. He found the reptile populations of East African national parks—the world's land megafauna capitals—much scarcer than those in Central or South American ones. He theorized that the big game and their predators increased the population of smaller scavengers like jackals, foxes, and raptors, which then preyed heavily on snakes, lizards, and turtles at times when scavenging failed, such as droughts. Still, the Central and South American parks where Janzen found reptiles abundant have more diverse megafaunas than Bay Area ones, including reptile eaters like peccaries, jaguars (which relish turtles), jaguarundis, ocelots, tayras, and a wide range of vultures and raptors.

One thing is certain, anyway. If a place is big enough for elk and mountain lions, it's big enough for many other creatures. I've seen more

Pacific pond turtles in boar-infested Henry Coe than anywhere else in the Bay Area. And while reconstituted mammoths are unlikely in the Bay Area's foreseeable future, some monster mammals moving around the landscape would be a good counterpoint to the monster homes crawling up the hillsides.

—*Bay Nature*, January–March 2004

first impressions

The Bay Area has a long history of flower children. At least, that's what a portrait of Adelbert von Chamisso, who gave the California poppy its scientific name, suggests. His flowing locks and rakish beret wouldn't seem out of place on a Family Dog concert poster. In fact, Chamisso was a pioneer of the romanticism that later evolved into hippie poets and rock singers. Robert Schumann used his love poems as lyrics for his famous leider.

Born to French nobles who fled to Germany after the Revolution of 1789, Chamisso grew up speaking German and even served in the Prussian army, but he suffered from a sense of cultural alienation and confused identity. He expressed this in his poetry as well as a classic short story, "Peter Schlemihl," about a man who sells his shadow to the devil. His alienation also motivated him to study natural history. "Shut off from society by my early guilt," he wrote, "Nature, which I had ever loved, was given me for my enjoyment, spread out like a rich garden before me."

A romantic poet like Chamisso would be an unlikely expedition member today, but artists were as liable as scientists to become explorers in the early nineteenth century. Indeed, scientists per se didn't exist yet. The Swedish botanist Carl Linnaeus had only recently founded biology as a systematic discipline, and the word "scientist" wouldn't come into common use for decades. Germany's greatest poet, Goethe, was among its leading botanists. The natural world, increasingly accessible and still largely unknown, was open to anyone with the energy and curiosity to explore it. Though the expeditions they accompanied were colonial and commercial, artistic explorers like Chamisso sought beauty as well as facts. Early conservationists like Thoreau and Muir would be enthusiastic readers of their accounts.

In 1815, partly to avoid serving in another war against Napoleon, the thirty-four-year-old poet shipped aboard a Russian expedition led by a twenty-eight-year-old captain, Otto von Kotzebue. It circled the globe but paid special attention to western North America because Russia's highly profitable sea otter trade was threatened as more hunters competed for a dwindling population. In October 1816, Kotzebue's ship, the *Rurik*, sailed into San Francisco Bay, then so remote that the Spanish colony's garrison had never seen a Russian flag. The soldiers also hadn't been paid for seven years: they survived by buying food from the Franciscan mission with money made from smuggling.

"We ate on shore in a tent," Chamisso wrote in his journal, "and our friends from the Presidio were always promptly on hand. . . . The misery in which they languished . . . did not permit them to be hosts."

The orange poppies that are now the state flower were so abundant on coastal hills then that California was known as Tierra del Fuego. Spanish colonists called them lyrical names like *copa de oro* and *dormidera*, "little sleeper," referring to their use as a mild narcotic. But the Bay Area's very remoteness, along with Spain's suspicion of colonial rivals, made the *Rurik*'s stay so brief that Chamisso never saw poppies covering the hills, only stray late-blooming specimens. So, although he collected, described, and scientifically named it, the poppy's spring glories never made it into the romantic poems he wrote after returning to Europe.

Chamisso's truncated vision of the Bay Area's showiest flower reflects a paradox about the region. Although it is one of the world's largest and loveliest estuarine ecosystems, Old World civilization has tended to overlook its natural qualities—first because so few civilized people knew of it, then because so many did as they rushed to exploit it when the 1849 gold rush transformed it from a backwater to a boomtown.

Indeed, it took civilization more than two centuries to find San Francisco Bay. European ships began sailing up the California coast in the 1500s, but the foggy and seldom pacific Pacific Ocean seems to have hidden the Golden Gate during all that time, although early natural history accounts are scanty because conditions were too harrowing for educated observers, except the occasional ship's captain or priest. They sketch a kind of lost world where forbidding coastal climate hid bucolic conditions inland. The first Spanish expedition, captained by Juan Rodriguez Cabrillo in 1542, recorded snow on bleak hills above Monterey Bay in November but rich forests and savannas inland, with large human populations and herds of elk and pronghorns so numerous that they reminded the adventurers of livestock in Spain. But frequent violent storms and outbreaks of scurvy decimated the expedition. Wounded in a fight with native Costonoans, Cabrillo himself died of gangrene.

Although Cabrillo's ships sailed past the Bay Area, a more famous expedition probably stopped here to refit in 1579. Sir Francis Drake's *Golden Hind* certainly circumnavigated the globe, but most of what is known about his alleged stay here is from a book later published by his nephew. It is probably based on the expedition chaplain's journal, but some historians suspect it was partly fabricated to contravene Spain's America claims. Still, although some scholars advocate other sites, the book's natural history descriptions sound a lot like someplace on the Bay Area's coast—possibly Bodega Bay but more likely Drakes Bay at Point Reyes. It was almost certainly not San Francisco Bay; the crafty English pirates would have known a good thing if they'd seen it.

The Drake book mentions islands where the crew killed enough seals and seabirds to supply their voyage to Asia. They sound like the Farallones. It says that the native people made long formal speeches when the English arrived and later returned gifts they had been offered, while women wailed and scratched their faces until the blood ran. They sound like the Coast Miwoks native to Point Reyes, who believed that the spirits of their dead passed out to sea. When a whale-sized object full of pale, strangely clad men suddenly appeared offshore, the Miwoks may well have taken them for ancestral spirits.

Although it was June, the Drake book reports that "nipping cold" and "most stynkinge fogges" prevailed in the Bay and that "the face of the earthe itselfe" was "unhandsome and deformed . . . shewing trees without leaves, and the ground without greenes." Drakes Bay is often like that in summer, especially after fires. Inland, however, they found "a goodly counry" populated by "very large and fat Deere, which we saw by the thousands, as we supposed, in a hearde." The book doesn't describe local wildlife in detail, except "a strange kind of Connies," of which "the whole Countrey" was "a warren." With feet like a mole's, a tail like a rat's, and food-carrying pouches on either side of its head, the "connie" sounds like the pocket gopher, of which the Drakes Bay headlands are still "a warren."

Two more Spanish expeditions passed along the coast, in 1595 and 1602, but the declining empire then largely ignored Alta California for almost two centuries. European geographers mapped it as an island for most of that time. When the overland Gaspar de Portola expedition finally discovered San Francisco Bay from the East Bay hills in 1769, it was an accident—they were looking for already-known Monterey Bay.

The de Anza expedition, which arrived a few years later, did include an observant and articulate naturalist. Pedro Font, a native of Catalonia, was a missionary in northwest Mexico when his superiors ordered him to accompany de Anza, with whom he traveled overland, on horseback or foot, from the Colorado River to the Bay Area, where he spent part of March and April 1776. Like his predecessors, Font had mixed feelings about the place. He enjoyed the warm spring weather and wildflowers but disliked the rugged wildness of it. Grizzly bears terrified him: "There are many of these beasts in that country, and they often attack and do damage to the Indians when they go to hunt, of which I have seen horrible examples."

Coastal redwoods awed Font, but he was less impressed with the interior valleys' potential as places to establish missions, his main concern. "This place is one of very level land, well covered with pasturage," he wrote of the South Bay, "but it is lacking in firewood, for there is no timber but that along the river, which is of cottonwoods, sycamores, ash, and laurel; and in all that region there is not a single stone." The expedition ventured east through the Livermore Valley, but although the Sierra Nevada gleamed invitingly in the distance, the Central Valley marshes and alkali flats daunted even the intrepid de Anza. Font thought the country might be uninhabitable, certainly one of the great real estate misappraisals of all time.

Even after Spain established the San Francisco Presidio later in 1776, explorers continued to sail right past the Bay. But that was changing. Voyaging was safer, and the search for colonial wealth had become systematic as empires competed for territory. A British expedition to California under Captain George Vancouver entered the Bay three times between 1792 and 1794, so unnerving Spanish officials that they restricted the English to the Presidio.

Naturalists played an integral part in this, since wildlife like the sea otter could have enormous commercial value. The Vancouver expedition naturalist, Archibald Menzies, was a paragon of the new exploration. He would circumnavigate the globe twice during his career. English botany's doyen, Sir Joseph Banks, had enjoined him "to investigate the whole of the natural history of the countries visited, paying attention to the nature of the soil, and with the prospect of sending out settlers from England, whether grains, fruits, etc., cultivated in Europe are likely to thrive. All trees, shrubs, plants, grasses, ferns, and mosses are to be enumerated by their scientific names as well as those used in the language of the natives." Menzies complied energetically, and hundreds of his specimens—including redwood, California laurel, big-leaf maple, toyon, madrone (*Arbutus menziesii*), and Douglas fir (*Pseudotsuga menziesii*)—were the first of their kind to reach Europe.

Menzies's job on the expedition was not easy. He was on less than friendly terms with Vancouver, who turned his botanical assistant before the mast—made him work as a sailor instead of a plant collector—then put Menzies himself under arrest when he complained. Most of his live specimens (including roots and seeds of California poppy) died during the voyage, perhaps because he was unable to care for them with his assistant banished to the rigging. Like Chamisso, he missed the Bay Area's spring flowering season. "I had little opportunity to augment my botanical collection," he wrote of an October 1794 foray into Tomales Bay. "We saw no fresh water, and the arid aspect of the Country would indicate its being a scarce article if at all procurable."

Two decades later, when Chamisso sailed into the Bay on Kotzebue's *Rurik*, he faced similar difficulties, including strained relations with a domineering captain. He knew that Menzies had collected there—Vancouver's account of the voyage had appeared in 1798, although little had been published about its botanical discoveries. The Russians had aroused Spanish suspicions even more than the English by establishing Fort Ross north of Bodega Bay, so the authorities restricted the expedition to the Presidio even on its first visit. A trip to Mission Dolores, then an hour's ride inland, was the longest that Kotzebue recorded during the October stay.

"The fogs, which the prevailing sea winds blow over the coast, dissolve in summer over a heated and parched soil," Chamisso wrote, echoing Menzies's frustration, "and the country exhibits in autumn only the prospect of bare scorched tracts, alternating with poor stunted bushes, and dazzling wastes of drift sand . . . the Flora of this country is not adorned by one of those species of plants which are produced by a warmer sun."

But his poet's eye helped Chamisso see diversity in apparent monotony. "It however offers much novelty to the botanist," he continued. "Well known North American species are found mixed with others belonging to the country; and most of the kinds are yet undescribed." He eventually gave scientific names to more than thirty new plant species in San Francisco, including California wax myrtle, yerba buena, and California sagebrush, as well as California poppy. He named the latter *Eschscholzia californica,* after his friend Johann Eschscholtz, the expedition surgeon. Chamisso was the first to recognize the species's uniqueness—Menzies had placed it in an Old World poppy genus, the celandines. Again like Menzies, however, Chamisso had little success with live specimens.

The first botanist to send back many viable live specimens of California plants was David Douglas, a self-taught Scottish horticulturist who spent nineteen months in what was by then Mexican California, from 1830 to 1833. An energetic if moody man, Douglas was the first to climb many peaks in the Cascades and Rockies. California's unique vegetation fascinated him. He wrote an English patron: "It would take at least three years to do anything like justice to the botany." Douglas spent relatively little time in the Bay Area, but, characteristically, he saw much. He apparently climbed Mount Diablo and made discoveries there, including the endemic Mount Diablo globe lily. He described the redwoods, which he saw in the East Bay hills and on the San Francisco peninsula, as "the great beauty of California vegetation . . . which gives the mountains a most peculiar, I was almost going to say awful, appearance."

The 1848 Sutter's Mill gold discovery marked the end of natural history's romantic era in California. In its wake, the Bay Area changed in two years from a wilderness outpost to the West Coast's major metropolis, and minerals replaced living organisms as the focus of interest. The era was not inactive in biological research—it saw the founding of the California Academy of Sciences in 1853. But even a professional botanist like William H. Brewer had to get a job with the State Geological Survey, founded in 1861, to explore here. Appointed "principal assistant, in charge of the botanical department," Brewer spent as much time in the Bay Area investigating coal and mercury deposits as native plants.

Many native species had already disappeared from the region by that time. In the valleys west of Mount Diablo, where Font had seen flowery bunchgrass prairies thronged with wildlife, Brewer described a state of "high cultivation; farmhouses have sprung up and rich fields of grain and growing orchards abound. Game was once very abundant—and deer, antelope, and elk like cattle, in herds. . . . All are now exterminated, but we find their horns by the hundreds." Only in backcountry like Corral Hollow east of Livermore Valley did he see grizzlies and pronghorns, and they soon vanished there.

When John Muir reached San Francisco in 1868, he had heard so much about the area's wholesale urbanization that he asked the first man he met the quickest way out of town, then kept walking until he got to Yosemite Valley. Indeed, he was a little neglectful of the Bay Area's natural qualities after he settled in Martinez in 1880 to manage his father-in-law's fruit ranch. Except for jottings in his private journals, he wrote little about them.

Yet Muir's classic description of the Central Valley seen from Pacheco Pass on his way to Yosemite in 1868 shows how romantic natural history like Chamisso's had transformed perceptions. Where Font had seen only desolation a century before, Muir saw a landscape that "after all my wanderings still appears as the most beautiful I have ever beheld . . . glowing golden in the sunshine . . . one smooth, flowery, lake-like bed of fertile soil." Had Muir arrived in the Bay Area a few decades earlier, he could have described its' valley floor wildflowers similarly.

Early naturalists' visions of this place are dimmed, but they survive. Many of the wildflowers collected by Chamisso and Menzies still grow in the built-over Presidio. Botanists used explorers' descriptions to look for them, although not without difficulty. Alice Eastwood, a botanist with the California Academy of Sciences, wrote in the 1940s that "very few" of the species Chamisso described survived in the Presidio because "the dense forest of cypress, pine and eucalyptus planted years ago" had replaced them. But Eastwood's eye seems to have missed on that occasion. "Fortunately I did not know of these comments when I embarked on a search for these plants," wrote Ida Geary, another botanist, in a 1979 issue of *Fremontia*, the magazine of the California Native Plant Society. Inspired by the earlier accounts, Geary and her associates combed the Presidio and made surprising discoveries. "The first year [1976] we found 48 of the 82 [species that Eschscholtz and Chamisso collected] . . . recently, we added more." Geary's finds included rarities like dune tansy, a sunflower relative that grows only in the Bay Area, as well as survival experts like California poppy.

Today, habitat restoration projects at the Presidio aim to use early records as guides for restoring more of those species, although such efforts sometimes run up against people's desire for shady woodlands of exotic trees instead of natural open dunes—the "bare, scorched tracts" that Chamisso described. But his descriptions could lead to a better balance between the world that explorers found here and the world colonists brought with them.

—*Bay Nature*, January–March 2006

oaklands

I live in the Thousands Oaks district in Berkeley, but I don't know why it's called that. Did someone go around and count the oaks in the early twentieth century when it was becoming a suburb? I don't think so, but it's a nice round number for real estate promotion. And there must have been a lot of oaks here, probably well over a thousand, mostly coast live oaks and valley oaks along the creeks, with perhaps some blue oaks and interior live oaks on drier spots. Many original coast live oaks remain in out of the way places, and there may be some valley oaks too. I don't recall encountering any original blue oaks or interior live oaks, which live mainly farther inland.

I know of one very large interior live oak here, however. It's in the parking strip in front of my house, and I planted it twenty years ago to replace a dying ornamental cherry. It is so large, indeed, that I might have thought twice about planting it if I'd foreseen its size. Interior live oak tends to be smaller than coast live oak, but maybe that's because it mostly grows in drier places. My parking strip tree has found interior live oak heaven. It has grown bigger than a coast live oak across the street that was already mature when I planted it, perhaps abetted by the subterranean plume of sewer leaks that percolates down from the stately homes in the hills.

The tree has a certain unnerving air of urban legend. It's like a mutant monster movie oak, relentlessly reaching toward the house, the power lines above the street, and the pipes under the ground. It continually grimes my car with aphid gum and crisp little brown leaves. It repels the street sweeper with its branches. It lifts the sidewalk, although not as high as the exotic sweet gums and camphor trees on the rest of the block. Pruning just seems to encourage it. Tree removal companies leave business cards on the porch.

There are compensations. Bush tits build Christmas stocking nests in it. On late summer evenings, tree crickets sing in it, audible from houses away. (They don't sing in the camphor trees or sweet gums.) I don't know the half of what goes on in it related to crows, jays, nuthatches, titmice, woodpeckers, squirrels, bats, and so forth. Another compensation is less rational. In these days of media hand-wringing about sudden oak death and other tree scourges, I just like having an overgrown native oak in front of my house, figuratively thumbing its nose at the socioeconomic growth engine that sheds crocodile tears about tree diseases as it condones their invasion.

For good or ill, not all oaks are so vigorous. Another tree that I planted in the parking strip at the same time as the live oak seemed likely to be a fast grower. It came from a big acorn that I found under an oracle oak, a hybrid of interior live oak and California black oak that appears frequently enough to have a name. Oracle oaks are evergreen like interior live oaks, but their leaves have spiny lobes like black oaks.

Hybrids tend to be vigorous, and the acorn I picked up certainly was. When I got home, I dropped it in a pot with some humus and forgot about it awhile. When I looked again, its taproot had grown around and around the pot, looking for a way out. So I planted it, and it grew fast at first, but, although it's still alive, its trunk is about a quarter of the size of the interior live oak's trunk. A fungus attacks its branches and foliage every year. Anyway, it's not an oracle oak. It's deciduous, and although its lobed leaves are spiny like a black oak's, the lobes are broader, like a Garry oak's. I don't know what to call it.

But that's not unusual with oaks. In fact, we'll probably never be sure how many kinds of oaks there are. Global estimates of oak species numbers range from two hundred to one thousand, and just about ever source I've consulted cites a different number. Oaks have been "speciating" for many millions of year, and, as I discovered in my parking strip, the various species readily hybridize to form crosses that may or may not be species, depending on taxonomists and geneticists. Even the genus itself, *Quercus*, seems shaky. Several decades ago some new trees turned up in Malaysia, and scientists had trouble deciding if they belonged in *Quercus* or not. Some well-known trees in East Asia and

North America are classed in different genera but are called oaks, like the tanoaks in the North Bay. Tanoaks bear odiferous white flowers like those of chestnuts (genus *Castanea*), but their nuts are like acorns, not chestnuts, so we call them oaks, although their genus is *Lithocarpus*, "stone seed." Oak death is hard on tanoaks; another fungus virtually extirpated American chestnut from Appalachian forests.

All this taxonomy indicates the oaks' importance. The more something concerns people, the more names they have for it. Oaks are *the* hardwoods of temperate forest; no other broadleaf genus is more widely distributed or abundant. Oaks dominate not only the temperate deciduous forests of the Northern Hemisphere but the temperate evergreen ones as well. They invaded South America and Africa as land bridges formed, and they followed Western civilization to Australia and New Zealand.

Quercus may have a leaf style for every gradation of temperate sunlight; it certainly has one for every Bay Area gradation. At one extreme, big, soft, floppy leaves absorb every filtered sunbeam on canyon bottoms; at the other, tiny, hard, waxy leaves resist chaparral's relentless heat and light. Individual plants produce a variety of shapes and textures adapted to conditions. In the full sunlight at the top of deciduous oaks, leaves are slender and deeply lobed, quite unlike their broad, shallow-lobed counterparts on lower branches. How the tree "knows" to do this is not well understood.

Temperate landscapes tend to be mosaics of oak diversity, with one or more species to a habitat, and the Bay Area is an example. Deciduous valley oak (*Q. lobata*) is prima donna, North America's largest oak, growing on sites with deep, well-drained soils and plenty of moisture— canyon bottoms, savannas, foothill flats. In the North Bay, the similar, slightly smaller Garry oak (*Q. garryana*) shares the hills with California black oak (*Q. kellogii*), Douglas fir, and tanoak. Coast live oak (*Q. agrifolia*) often shares habitat with these trees but is more adaptable, and it predominates throughout the ocean-side hills. Black oak also appears at higher elevations throughout the Bay Area, and if the slopes are steep and rocky enough, canyon live oak (*Q. chrysolepis*) does too.

As the habitat gets tougher, the oaks do. Interior live oak (*Q. wislilzennii*) tends to replace coast live oak on the slopes east of the ocean-side hills, and as the climate gets steadily hotter and drier toward the Central Valley, blue oak (*Q. douglassii*) becomes increasingly predominant, until it and ghost pine are virtually the only trees for miles. Although blue oak is winter deciduous like valley and black oak, it is even more resistant to arid climate than some desert shrubs such as mesquite and ironwood. During droughts, blue oaks undergo physiological changes that let them use decreasing amounts of water. When weather becomes too dry, they drop their leaves in summer and stay dormant until the next spring.

If conditions are even more stressful, oaks readily trade their arche-typical tree status for survival as shrubs. In the Bay Area, several kinds of shrub oak live happily in dry, windswept chaparral and can be hard to distinguish from *real* shrubs like mountain mahogany, silktassel, and (of course) poison oak. It's also hard to distinguish them from each other, not least in that both coast and interior live oak have stunted forms that grow in chaparral. The University of California Press *Native Shrubs of the Bay Area* says, "At least two" local species "can truly be called shrubs": leather oak (*Q. durata*) and scrub oak (*Q. berberidifolia*). But I've never been very clear about them. Both species are known to hybridize not only with valley oak and Garry oak but with each other.

The Bay Area's abundance and diversity of oaks had a lot to do with the high density of Native American populations here. Acorns were their staff of life, and if the crops of the most desirable species, tanoak, failed, there were always valley and coast live oaks, and then black oak and the other oaks. It's less clear what the effect of the high human density on the oaks was. Much of the Bay Area was grassland when Europeans arrived, with woodland scattered in hills, in canyons, and along streams. Woods were so scattered in the East and South Bay that there is no historical record of tree squirrels; the native gray squirrel is still confined to the North Bay. Whether hundreds of generations of people gathering acorns had something to do with this is impossible to say. Native Americans certainly treasured oaks: a family's right to gather from specific groves was passed from generation to generation.

If native people possibly reduced oak woodland gradually, colonists certainly did so quickly. With no use for acorns except as livestock food, they had little reason to conserve the trees. As whaling, fur hunting, and the hide trade between Spanish cattle barons and Yankee merchantmen burgeoned in the early nineteenth century, coast live oaks disappeared with accelerating speed into the boilers and stoves of ships as well as of colonial towns. Mission environs described as live oak woodlands by the founding Franciscans in the late eighteenth century were treeless by the 1830s.

Spanish and then Mexican colonists used oak for barrels, wagons, tools, and furniture. They didn't use much for building. Like the Southwest, California was a land of adobe and brick before loggers pushed north to the big conifer forests. Valley oak is brittle and relatively soft—called mush oak by some—and live oak wood, although strong, is generally too knotty for boards. Plenty of strong, straight Garry oaks grew in the North Bay, but native people there resisted colonization until the surge of Anglo invasion. Anyway, those oaks grew with such a wealth of conifers that they were bypassed when logging began in earnest.

Bay Area history since then has been grim for oaks, as ranching, farming, and urbanization destroyed most of the habitat. Oaks are more at risk than redwoods, especially valley oaks, which grow in prime subdivision areas. Even if they're left standing, summer watering of lawns and gardens kills them through root diseases. Oaks seem to be having trouble reproducing even in nonurbanized areas. One can walk for hours through mature oak woodland and see very few saplings. Many creatures eat the acorns, and many attack the seedlings that manage to sprout. One study suggested that rodent populations increased by introduction of exotic grasses and forbs were suppressing oak reproduction. Others blamed deer and livestock. Blue oak seedlings in particular tend to have a nibbled look about them.

Attempts to help oaks reproduce by planting saplings in plastic sleeves seem to have limited success. Many of the trees thus protected at Mount Diablo in the 1990s have not survived, perhaps partly because the state stopped maintaining them as funding dried up. Sometimes the sleeves even harmed the trees instead of protecting them, as with a blue oak sapling I found that had been bowed to the ground when its sleeve collapsed. I propped it up, but it declined slowly over the next two years. Oak growth is a lengthy process in this climate.

Considering how oaks reproduce, simply by dropping a large, nutritious seed on the ground, it may seem surprising that *Quercus* has survived for millions of years. This suggests that we don't really understand the dynamics of oak regeneration. Despite the apparently dismal prospects, oaks are reproducing here. Coast live oaks in particular are determined hangers-on in urban areas, coming up in hedges, fence lines, and so on. They are just as ubiquitous in the hills. The other species are less resilient, but the more I look, the more seedlings and saplings of valley oak, blue oak, interior live oak, and black oak I see.

Little Yosemite in Pine Canyon at Mount Diablo is a kind of Bay Area oak hologram, with valley oaks on the flats; coast live oaks by the creeks; interior live oaks, black oaks, and blue oaks on the slopes and ridgelines; and scrub oaks in the chaparral around Castle Crags, although I don't know if they are the real chaparral species or just stunted live oaks. But that uncertainty seems typical of oaks too.

I never get tired of the seasonal leaf color changes there: from catkin pink to yellow-green to dark bluish green to autumn violet and amber to winter violet. It has a tapestry quality, like the backgrounds of Italian Renaissance portraits. Pine Canyon really should be called Oak Canyon—the pines are just scatterings of ghost pines. But almost every canyon in the Bay Area would be an Oak Canyon if that were the main naming criterion.

—2008

dance of the webspinners

Alien species are so controversial—as with the endless squabbles about eucalyptus trees—that the idea of exotic organisms invading the Bay Area and having no discernible environmental impacts seems counterintuitive. But a couple of exotic species here are so ecologically unassuming as to be virtually unnoticed. When Santa Clara University's magazine asked me to contribute an article on the subject, I'd never heard of them.

The editor wanted me to write about a biology professor who studies webspinners, so I assumed he was talking about spiders. I was wrong. Webspinners, technically called embiids, are insects, and they comprise an entire order. Like tent caterpillars, they live colonially in webs that they spin out of the strong, sticky proteins that we call silk, but the similarity ends there. Tent caterpillars are the larvae of moths, among the world's best-known insects. Embiids may not be the world's least-known insects, but they are serious contenders for the title. Their closest relatives, according to Janice Edgerly-Rooks, who studies them at Santa Clara, are the stick insects that weirdly mimic branches or leaves. But embiids don't look or behave quite like anything else.

"Their bodies are very elongated because they spend most of their lives in their colonies," Edgerly-Rooks said. "Earwigs are about the only common insects I can think of to compare them to, but that's terrible because people hate earwigs, and embiids don't act like earwigs, infesting houses and pinching. Embiids are about as inoffensive as insects get."

Until scientists got interested in them, humans virtually ignored embiids. They don't eat anything we want or otherwise interfere with us.

Various species feed directly on lichens, leaf litter, soil detritus, and other humble plant materials. We haven't found much use for embiids either. Their silk isn't woven into fabric as with silkworm moth cocoons or some tropical spiderwebs. Even where people eat insects, embiids aren't on the menu. The only use Edgerly-Rooks knew about is in Central America, where people make bandages from embiid webs. (Antibiotic chemicals in the silk may help to prevent infections.)

Of course, embiids' economic unimportance to humans doesn't mean they are unimportant in nature. "The first thing people usually ask me about embiids is what they are good for," Edgerly-Rooks said. "I could ask what humans are good for compared to embiids, which play a big ecological role in converting plant detritus into soil. If they all disappeared, we don't know what would happen."

Embiids are an ancient order, occurring on every continent except Antarctica, but they seem never to have adapted to cool climates, and most species live in the tropics. The few species native to the United States occur in the Southeast or along the Mexican border. Civilization is changing that, however, as climate warms and some embiids hitch rides on ships and other transport. Although the Bay Area has no native embiids, two genera have colonized it within the past century. The nimble, cryptic insects take advantage of suburban growth: "They spin their webs in mulch or other stuff used in landscaping," Edgerly-Rooks said, "so the more people move the stuff around, the more embiids they get. I just found webs in the mulch around a new parking lot outside the lab here."

One genus, *Haploembia*, is from the Mediterranean and is now common here, spinning bluish webs under rocks. The other genus, *Oligotoma*, comes from the Middle East and is scarcer than *Haploembia*, suggesting that it arrived later. But it reproduces faster, so it will probably increase. It has colonized many other countries, sometimes to Edgerly-Rooks's chagrin when she travels in search of new embiids and finds that *Oligotoma* has arrived before her.

Embiids are indeed inconspicuous. My own attempts to find wild Bay Area colonies by turning over rocks were flops. Even when Edgerly-Rooks showed me captive colonies in her laboratory, the clear plastic containers just seemed full of dead leaves until she pointed out networks of tubular webs on their sides. When she opened a canister, it looked lifeless inside until she began lifting leaves and revealing slender brown shapes with oddly enlarged front legs that swiftly scurried out of sight. "Embiid" derives from the Greek for "lively." Their cryptic grace made them seem elfin, like something in *A Midsummer Night's Dream*.

She had pinned a sliver of persimmon to the leaves as a treat, although the embiids can live on just leaf litter. When I asked how many were in the canister, she shook her head: "I don't know. Hundreds." The lab's dozens of canisters doubtless contained many thousands of embiids, all munching happily on dead leaves and a little persimmon and lettuce. Some colonies have thrived for years since she collected them in the wild.

She had about thirty species from many bioregions, and they demonstrated what is perhaps most unusual about the order. Her species all looked pretty much alike, and in fact *all* the world's embiid species look pretty much alike: "You can look at females of five different species together and not see any differences except maybe in the color. There may be subtle variations, and the eggs can be shaped differently, but on the whole there's an amazing uniformity of appearance. They're the only insect order like that."

On the other hand, Edgerly-Rooks said, embiid behavior may be unusually diverse and complex. "When I sent embiid behavioral data to a software specialist, he told me it was the 'longest repeating pattern' he'd ever seen. They're not machines. If something happens to their web, they go with their antennae and evaluate the situation and find out what needs to be done and start doing it."

Embiids are also unusual in that they spin their silk from multiple glands in their enlarged front feet instead of from their mouths like caterpillars. A David Attenborough documentary, *Life in the Undergrowth*, shows an embiid on a rain forest tree on the Caribbean island of Trinidad spinning silk to repair a hole in her colony. Again, there is something elfin about this—it's like Jack Frost painting a windowpane. "You can't really see it on the screen, but she was literally bending over backwards to spin," Edgerly-Rooks, who helped with the film, said. "Embiids appear to do yoga. Most adult insects are built like tanks and have limited or no flexibility. It's kind of like wearing a coat of armor. It would be hard to do yoga with that kind of body."

All embiids, male and female, adult and immature, spin the silken tubes wherein they spend most of their lives, but spinning behavior varies. Some species spin more silk than others, and different species have different spinning patterns. Edgerly-Rooks called the patterns "choreographies," and the intricate, rhythmic ways that the little insects waved their legs to produce and distribute the silk did seem like dancing. Embiid species that live in soil or leaf litter tend to spin just enough silk to make their tubes and form small colonies. Species that live aboveground on tree trunks or rocks may spin protective sheet webs over their tubes, and the sheets can shield large colonies. Embiid silk varies in color from brilliant white to blue or pink, and large above ground colonies can be easily visible to people who know about embiids. People who don't know about embiids tend not to notice even large colonies, or to assume that spiders spin them.

As with most insects, embiid females are the main players in the life cycle. Wingless and sedentary, they make the colonies. Female care of eggs and young, generally uncommon among insects, is a basic trait of the Embiidina. Unlike termites or ants, however, embiid colonies don't have hierarchies and division of labor. They are groups of females that live together because it helps them to guard their eggs and babies (called nymphs, since they hatch resembling small adults instead of as worm-like larvae). On reaching maturity, young individuals usually leave their natal colony and join another or establish one of their own.

Edgerly-Rooks wrote her PhD dissertation on female natal care at the Asa Wright Field Station on Trinidad. "Because the British had owned the island, there was a big natural history literature, so it seemed like a good place to study them. When I got to the field station, I found colonies all over the trees. But nobody knew much about them, so I'd take an umbrella into the rain forest and watch embiids all day. And I soon found out one reason why the females guard their eggs in colonies.

"There are little wasps that parasitize embiid eggs by laying their own eggs inside them. Whenever I was at an embiid colony, the wasps were waiting around within the silk. And whenever the web got torn for any reason, the wasps mobilized to attack the embiid eggs, because the mother embiid was distracted by her repair work. So if the female embiids weren't guarding their eggs all the time, they lost them. And it took six weeks for the eggs to hatch; that whole time the maternal females had little time to feed themselves, because they were always on guard duty. So I could see one 'why' of embiid social behavior. As soft-bodied, sedentary animals, embiids are very vulnerable to predators."

Edgerly-Rooks paused, then clarified: "Actually, the adults aren't all that vulnerable, because they can run really fast, and they can run backward even faster than forward. They can do incredibly fast inside-out

U-turns. But the eggs and nymphs are easy targets. So there's a selective advantage for females to join with each other because something like a wasp is less likely to get into a colony if many females are maintaining it than if just a few are." There are trade-offs to forming big colonies, though. "The bigger the embiid colonies get, and the longer they last, the more wasps and other predators they attract."

Embiid males resemble male ants, in that they exist mainly to mate. They search for colonies of females with chemoreceptors on their elongated antennae, and when they find one, they try to get inside the silk tubes, often facing resistance from the female residents, as well as competition from other males. A male that finds a willing female performs a courtship ritual that involves twining his body around her. Embiid males are winged in some species, wingless in others. Winged males don't feed after maturity, so their lives are brief. Wingless males continue to feed and may move into colonies to keep other males away. In some species, such males have enlarged heads, which may help them guard the females. Some other males of such species are slimmer and may mimic females as a way to get around the big-headed males in competition for mates.

Some embiid species have dispensed with males altogether and are parthenogenetic—a Greek and Latin cognate word meaning "virgin birth." The females produce nymphs—always female—without mating. Entomologists once thought that the commoner Bay Area immigrant embiid, *Haploembia*, was a single parthenogenetic species, but then males turned up in Palo Alto and Mountain View. So Edgerly-Rooks thinks there may be two *Haploembia* species here—one with males and one without.

Embiid males are vital to science because the shapes of their genitalia are among the few features by which taxonomists can distinguish at least the sexual species. "Another reason that embiids are obscure," Edgerly-Rooks wryly complained, "is that most field guides just illustrate them with a squashed male on a slide."

Although embiids aren't especially diverse by insect standards, there may be as many as two thousand species in fourteen families. Edgerly-Rooks has found a lot of species in the three decades she's been studying them. One of her main problems has been that ones she wanted to study weren't classified: "I'd take specimens to Ed Ross, a ninety-three-year-old taxonomist at the California Academy of Science who has named most of the embiid species known today. And he'd say: 'Oh, that's a can of worms. I haven't gotten to that yet.' So I wound up describing and naming species myself."

Edgerly-Rooks has embarked on a "life-changing" study of the relationship between embiid behavior and evolution funded by the National Science Foundation. Collaborating with a taxonomist and a molecular biologist, she has been observing embiids from all over the world: "The evolution of a group of organisms has usually been studied through its morphology," she said, "through is physical organization. But since embiids all look so similar, but have such complex behavior, it raises the question as to whether we can look at an organism's evolution through its behavior as well as its morphology.

"For example, how have all the different web-spinning choreographies that embiids perform evolved? Can we categorize groups of embiids by their spinning choreographies and perhaps see how spinning behavior might have affected evolution from one group to another—what we call phylogeny? And then, how has spinning affected the evolution of their social behavior? Embiids are a 'primitively social' order, so they may show us a lot about how organisms evolve social behavior in the first place."

As she scurried around her lab—from the embiid colonies to a computer, to another computer and back to the colonies—demonstrating the vast array of films, charts, statistics, and other data that she and her co-workers have amassed, Edgerly-Rooks began to seem a little embiid-like herself, using a technological choreography to spin a complex web of ideas and information. The concept of a human with embiid qualities wasn't new to her:

"Spider Man is really Embiid Man, you know," she said. "He spins his silk from his front appendages like an embiid." She waved her hands to demonstrate the embiid technique. "If he spun it from the tip of his abdomen like a spider, it would look pretty weird in the movies."

—*Santa Clara Magazine*, Spring 2009

salamander land

the marvelous caudata

In the 1980s, the BBC produced a nature series about North America called *Land of the Eagle.* The title is charismatic, but it makes little sense biologically. Our two eagle species belong to genera common elsewhere: Europe alone has four genera and ten species of resident and migratory eagles, including both of North America's genera. The BBC series should have been called *Land of the Salamander,* because North America has more kinds of salamanders—the tailed, mostly four-legged amphibians of the order Caudata—than any other continent, and some of our species are very like ancient ones, suggesting that the order may have arisen on some ancestral version of our continent.

I wasn't aware of our salamander supremacy when growing up in New England, but they were my favorites in the *Golden Nature Guide to Reptiles and Amphibians.* Finding such secretive but colorful little creatures under logs or in ponds fascinated me. Local red-backed salamanders and red-spotted newts were like old friends, while distant kinds seemed exotic. Down south, blind salamanders inhabited caves, and other species with outlandish names—hellbenders, mud puppies, sirens, congo eels—lurked in streams and swamps. Out west lived giant, worm, tiger, and tree salamanders, the last of which particularly caught my imagination.

"The Tree Salamander of the Pacific Coast frequently lives in water soaked cavities of trees," said the guide. "Sometimes a whole colony is found in one of these holes, where eggs are laid, also." A picture showed elfin creatures climbing around in hilly oak savanna. Another book said they been found sixty feet up in red tree vole nests and that as many as twenty-five lived in one colony. Another said they had prehensile tails, like opossums. They seemed marvelous.

Childhood fascinations can be disappointing in adulthood, but this one wasn't. I first arrived in on the Pacific Coast one rainy night in December 1968. Driving from San Francisco Airport north through Marin County, I saw little creatures crossing the road. When I pulled over for a closer look, I saw that they were tree salamanders just like those in the *Golden Guide*, only better: the headlights showed iridescent gold-and-silver mottling on their skins, where the book had shown drab brown.

I was immediately sold on a place where an early fascination could be so quickly fulfilled—or partly fulfilled. In the past decades I've seen many tree salamanders, now more commonly called arboreal salamanders (*Aneides lugubris*). They inhabit my garden in Berkeley. I've never actually seen one in a tree, but that would involve climbing the hollow, rotten ones they frequent on rainy nights. I prefer to take their arboreal side on faith. The idea of salamanders in trees still seems marvelous.

Salamander marvels go back a long way. Ancient European legends hold that *Salamandra salamandra*, a species related to newts, can live in fire because of its bright black-and-yellow markings and because individuals sometimes crawl out of logs in fireplaces. Asian lore says that salamanders of mountain lakes can control the weather—a source of dragon legends. California Native American mythology also ascribes magical power to mountain lake salamanders. Some are thought to protect water purity. Not all Bay Area species have acquired such mythic grandeur, but their evolutionary adaptations are pretty marvelous.

Arboreal salamanders belong to a family called the Plethodontidae, "many-toothed," because they have so many tiny teeth. They are also called lung-less salamanders because, unlike other kinds, they have lost their lungs in the course of their evolution. (The lobe-finned fish from which amphibians evolved had lungs.) Many of these lung-less species live entirely terrestrial lives, which may seem odd, since salamanders that do have lungs spend part or all of their lives in water. But plethodontids thrive on land by absorbing oxygen through their moist skins and mouths.

Plethodontids are like most other kinds of salamanders in that they mate by internal fertilization—of a specialized sort. Instead of injecting sperm into a female, a male secretes it into a gelatinous packet called a spermatophore, which he deposits in front of the female after attracting her by doing little dances (called *leibspiel*) or rubbing a sexually stimu-lating gland on his chin against her snout. If this foreplay is adequate, she picks up the spermatophore with her cloaca and it dissolves inside her and fertilizes her eggs. (It isn't always adequate. I've seen breeding places dotted with rejected spermatophores.)

Plethodontids differ from all other salamanders, however, in the way their young develop after fertilization. Like most frog tadpoles, the gilled larvae of most salamander families need to live in water as they develop into adults after hatching. But plethodontids go through the gilled larval stage in the egg and hatch as tiny versions of their lung-less, gill-less par-ents. Some plethodontid genera are semiaquatic, living on the edges of streams and springs: the females lay their eggs in water. Some are fully terrestrial: the females lay their eggs underground, often guarding them until they hatch. This uniquely terrestrial group is the most numerous and diverse one in North America, and it has produced the planet's only tropical salamanders by invading Central and South America and evolving over a hundred species there. Some of these take their arboreal lifestyle to extremes, spending their lives in the rain forest canopy.

Since the group overran America so successfully, it would seem logical that they'd overrun Eurasia too. But Old World plethodontids are rare. One genus known from Italy and southern France, *Hydro-mantes*, is related to species halfway across the globe here in the Sierra Nevada and Cascades. Herpetologists scratch their heads about that. UC–Berkeley professor David Wake, an authority on salamander evolu-tion, has posited from genetic evidence that plethodontids originated in North America and spread into Eurasia during the Cretaceous period, the late dinosaur age. *Hydromantes* may have evolved in Eurasia, then spread back into western North America.

Hydromantes was the only known Eurasian plethodontid until 2005, when an Illinois high school teacher, Stephen Karsen, turned over a rock in South Korea and found a completely new one, named *Karsenia ko-reana*. Herpetologists *really* scratch their heads about that. Finding a new vertebrate species is always unusual; finding a rare new genus in such a strangely isolated location is almost unprecedented. David Wake, who described the species, calls it "the most exciting and unexpected discovery of my career." Other new plethodontids keep turning up in America. The same year as *Karsenia*'s discovery, herpetologists de-scribed a new species, the Scott's Bar salamander, *Plethodon asupak,* in northern California. Wake and his colleagues described two new species in the southern Sierra Nevada in 2012.

All Bay Area plethodontid species are fully terrestrial, which is why, unlike water-breeding amphibians, some of them survive in my garden. Arboreal salamanders aren't even the most numerous ones there. The California slender salamander, *Batrachoseps attenuatus*, is almost as ubiquitous as the earthworm. It is also called the worm salamander because of its elongated body and tiny legs. Both arboreals and slenders prefer to keep out of sight, but I know they're here during winter rains when I put out recycling bins for collection. Arboreals sometimes hide underneath, and I often find several slenders coiled there like tiny snakes.

Given their numbers just in my yard, arboreal and slender salamander numbers in the region must be staggering. A 1956 study of geographic variation in both species on islands in the Bay estimated populations of seven thousand slender salamanders and nineteen hundred arboreals per acre on little Red Rock Island just south of the Richmond Bridge. (Sea level's rise after the last ice age probably isolated the salamanders on the islands—arboreals inhabit even the Farallones twenty-seven miles offshore—although they may have arrived by "waif disperal" on floating debris.)

Our superabundant plethodontids play a big part in the ecosystem, particularly since they are edible. Predators from bears to shrews eat them; I once found an arboreal salamander faced off against a robin on a Berkeley doorstep. Arboreals can bite hard with their tiny teeth, so I don't know which would have won if my arrival hadn't scared the robin away. Like lizards, salamanders can escape predators by losing their tails. They then grow new ones, and, unlike other vertebrates, they can even grow new limbs.

Like all salamanders, plethodontids are predators and eat incalculable numbers of invertebrates. Salamanders hunt mainly by sight, which is surprising considering their mainly nocturnal habits. They have color vision and can see into the ultraviolet end of the spectrum. Aquatic species also detect prey with a vibration-sensing lateral line organ inherited from fish ancestors. Salamander hearing is probably not good. They lack external ears and have only vestigial inner ears.

Not all Bay Area plethodontids are easy to find. Another *Aneides* subspecies, the Santa Cruz black salamander (*A. flavipunctatus niger*), occurs in the South Bay, but its habitat needs are more specialized: it prefers moist forest environments such as stream sides. Probably because of this specialization, the Santa Cruz subspecies is isolated from another black salamander, *A. f. flavipunctatus*, which occurs from Sonoma to Del Norte County. I've never seen it.

I have seen members of the other plethodontid genus that lives here, *Ensatina*, although never in urban areas. But they can be persistent in natural areas. There was a certain log beside the creek in Redwood Regional Park under which, for several years, I could be sure of greeting one *Ensatina* individual. Nobody knows why *Ensatina* shuns urbanization—or why slender and arboreal salamanders don't.

David Wake suspects that despite its distaste for civilization, the local *Ensatina* subspecies, the yellow-eyed salamander (*E. escholtzi xanthopicta*), is second only to the slender salamander in Bay Area numbers. A unique trait may help explain this. Its coloring, brown on top and orange underneath with yellow eye markings, is very like that of the California newt (*Taricha torosa*), which has highly toxic skin. When disturbed, yellow-eyed salamanders even mimic newt behavior by assuming postures that display their orange undersides. This may be an example of Batesian mimicry, whereby an edible animal evolves through natural selection to resemble a poisonous one.

Taricha newt skin is lethal because it contains an alkaloid called tetrodotoxin, which is more poisonous than cyanide. The story of campers who died from accidentally boiling one in their morning coffeepot is an urban legend that happens to be true. Mature *Taricha*'s only known predator is the garter snake, *Thamnophis*, some individuals of which can metabolically neutralize the poison. *Taricha* newt toxicity varies by location: the Bay Area is a hot spot, perhaps because local garter snakes developed an unusual immunity to the toxins, touching off a biological "arms race."

A student of Wake's, Shawn Kuchta, studied *Ensatina* mimicry on lands owned by the East Bay Municipal Utility District, putting out several hundred plasticine models of the yellow-eyed salamander and of another *Ensatina* subspecies, the Oregon salamander (*E. e. oregonensis*), which lives farther north and has a beige belly and black eyes—nothing like a newt. The experiment showed that, although the Oregon salamander's coloration makes it less conspicuous than the yellow-eyed, predators attacked twice as many of the Oregon models as the yellow-eyed ones. In other experiments, captive scrub jays prudently preferred Oregon salamanders to yellow-eyed ones. Several other *Ensatina* subspecies overlap with the California newt's range, but none mimic the newt in the same way. That is something else herpetologists scratch their heads about.

Batesian mimics tend to be shyer than the toxic organisms they imitate, and yellow-eyed salamanders follow this rule. They largely come out at night, whereas California newts are a frequent daytime sight here in the rainy season. The newt family, the Salamandridae, is the world's most widely distributed salamander family, occurring in North America, Eurasia, and North Africa. California newts live along the coast, from Humboldt to San Diego Counties and in the Sierra Nevada. The Bay Area also has another species, the rough-skinned newt (*T. granulosa*), which occurs from British Columbia south to Santa Cruz County.

Poisonous skin probably has a lot to do with newt success because, unlike plethodontids, they need water for breeding. Our newts are adaptable and occupy a variety of waters, from vernal pools to lakes and streams. At higher altitudes, they winter underground and summer in water: some mountain lake populations have learned to prey on backpackers by biting abraded skin cells from waders' feet. (It just tickles.)

Bay Area newt adults spend the dry summer months underground in places like ground squirrel burrows and move to water during winter rains. Males enter first and develop aquatic features—their skin gets smoother; their tails broaden and get more fin-like. As females arrive, the males are ready to compete for them and do so vigorously. Ponds teem with "newt balls" as gangs of sex-crazed males engulf females. A winner clasps a female behind her front legs and strokes her snout with his sexual stimulant gland, then swims in front of her and deposits his spermatophore. She lays her fertilized eggs in clusters that she attaches to water plants or submerged twigs. The gilled larvae hatch, grow, and move to land within a few months.

Newt larvae are shyer than adults because their skin poison hasn't developed. (Some biologists think adults acquire the toxin by ingesting bacteria that metabolize it.) The only place in the Bay Area where I've seen newt larvae was a shady, sandy-bottomed corner of a vernal pond at Henry Coe State Park. The pale, red-gilled creatures seemed fragile compared to their robust, lascivious parents, but newts remain common, so the larvae must be good at catching aquatic invertebrates and avoiding predators like giant water beetles and dragonfly nymphs. Introducing game fish into ponds or lakes can extirpate newt populations, however, along with other amphibians.

The Bay Area's two other salamander families occur only in North America. They depend on water for reproduction and are not poisonous; they survive by staying out of sight. Our most spectacular species, classified in a family by itself, is the Pacific giant salamander (*Dicamptodon ensatus*), which can grow to twelve inches. Santa Cruz County is at the southern extent of its range, since it prefers heavy forest, and adults are a rare sight in daytime. Their sexual privacy policy is the opposite of that of the newts. They mate largely in underground springs, where they also lay their eggs. On the other hand, their gilled larvae can be easy to see in clear forest streams, since they may grow to adult length before they mature and move underground.

The other Bay Area family is the Ambystomidae, which is our most vulnerable group because local species have special habitat needs. The tiger salamander, named for its yellow-and-black blotches, occurs in much of North America, but the California species (*Ambystoma californiense*) is isolated from the others. It favors grassland, breeding in vernal pools and stream oxbows, which are increasingly rare in the Bay Area. Remaining populations live mainly in nature preserves and wildlife refuges. The Sonoma County population is listed as endangered, and populations in the East Bay and Santa Clara County are considered threatened.

My *Golden Guide* didn't mention the rarest of all salamander species here—the long-toed salamander (*Ambystoma macrodactylum*). Various subspecies occurring from British Columbia to northeast California are fairly common, but the Santa Cruz salamander (*A. m. croceum*) breeds in only twenty or so sites in northern Monterey and southern Santa Cruz County. It wasn't discovered until 1954, and CALTRANS threatened it in the 1960s by bulldozing an important breeding pond while widening Highway 1. Surviving near a major highway and other developments, it too is on the endangered list.

Natural climate change probably caused the isolation of the California tiger salamander, Santa Cruz black salamander, and Santa Cruz long-toed salamander. During the cooler, wetter ice age, suitable habitat would have connected Bay Area populations with others to the east and north. As weather warmed and dried, habitat loss presumably extirpated populations in between. David Wake thinks changing climates caused the spotty distribution of many other salamander species. He fears that rapid human-caused climate change will combine with habitat destruction, pollution, and other factors to extirpate more salamander populations.

On the other hand, salamanders have been around hundreds of millions of years, whereas civilization has existed for five thousand. According to some computer models, global civilization's resource demands will exceed supply in about a hundred years, a dim prospect for "sustainable growth." So I wouldn't count salamanders out. If, as prophesied, the world ends in fire instead of flood next time, their mythic reputation for creeping out of the flames alive may prove true.

—*Bay Nature*, January–March 2013

AUTHOR'S NOTE: *A reader who had worked for UC–Berkeley's grounds crew noted that they often found arboreal salamanders in campus trees.*